ELIZABETH

ARDEN
Cosmetics Entrepreneur

ELIZABETH
ARDEN
Cosmetics Entrepreneur

By

Nancy Shuker

✳

T H E   A M E R I C A N   D R E A M

SILVER BURDETT PRESS
ENGLEWOOD CLIFFS, NEW JERSEY

Text © 1989 by Silver Burdett Press

Designed and produced by Blackbirch Graphics, Inc.

Project Editor: Nancy Furstinger

Manufactured in the United States of America

(Lib. ed.)   10   9   8   7   6   5   4   3   2   1

(Paper ed.)   10   9   8   7   6   5   4   3   2   1

Library of Congress Cataloging-in-Publication Data

Shuker, Nancy.
    Elizabeth Arden / by Nancy Shuker.
      (The American dream)
    Bibliography: p. 108
    Includes index.
    1. Arden, Elizabeth, 1878-1966. 2. Women in business—United States—Biography. 3. Cosmetics industry—United States—History.
    I. Title.   II. Series: American Dream (Englewood Cliffs, N.J.)
HD9970.5.C672A737 1988
338.7'6164672'09—dc19   88-29824
[B]   CIP
                                                      AC

ISBN 0-382-09587-1 (lib. bdg.)
ISBN 0-382-09595-2 (pbk.)

Contents

Young Florence Nightingale Graham returned to her father's small farm near Woodbridge, Ontario, after a semester of nursing school in the 1890s.

Chapter 1

Growing into a Name

*T*he woman who would win fame and fortune as Elizabeth Arden was born on New Year's Eve, 1878, in the tiny Canadian village of Woodbridge, Ontario. Perhaps her arrival at the turn of a new year was the reason that her birth filled her parents, Susan and William Graham, with particular hope.

It certainly wasn't the fact that she was a girl—and the third girl at that. In that era it was sons who were expected to bring pride to a family name, and her parents had only one.

Whatever it was, this baby girl was considered special. Picking a name for her became an important task for her mother and father.

Their son was named for his father, William Graham. The two other girls had been given pretty names that were popular at the time: Lillian and Christine.

The Grahams discussed many possibilities. They decided against naming her for the British queen, Victoria. So many girls had already been named for her. And they didn't want to name her for a famous actress, because such women were not considered to be respectable.

Suddenly, the new mother had an idea that she knew was right. Probably the most famous and well-regarded woman in the world in the late nineteenth century was an English nurse who had changed the way patients were treated in hospitals and had made a respected profession of caring for the sick. In 1854 she followed British troops to the Crimean War, and her work there proved that good nursing could save lives.

On her return to England she founded a school to train other women to be nurses. She believed good nursing care was a twenty-four-hour-a-day commitment and, despite frail health, often worked around the clock herself. Her name was Florence Nightingale.

The baby's mother had always admired this independent and heroic woman. Wouldn't it be wonderful if their new daughter could grow up to be like her?

"Florence Nightingale Graham," she said aloud just to try it. She liked the sound.

William thought it might be a hard name to live up to, but his wife was so enthusiastic that he went along with her.

"Florence Nightingale Graham it is!" he agreed.

Florence Nightingale Graham was blessed with a loving family, but not much else. Her father had been born in Scotland, the son of a tenant farmer. His father worked another man's land all his life, and young William grew up with a determination to change his own destiny.

William wanted to be a landowner and have the dignity of working for himself. His great love was horses, and he had a natural talent for training and riding the high-strung thoroughbreds that rich men raced. As he entered manhood, he already had won enough prize money as a rider to buy his own horse.

With his horse as his stake, he spent the spring months traveling the British Isles to the traditional county fairs that celebrated the end of winter. Horse races were a highlight of many of the fairs, with purses big enough to attract men like William from all over England and Scotland.

Florence's mother, Susan Tadd Graham, had grown up in Cornwall, on the southwest coast of England. Her grandfather, Samuel Tadd, had been master of the schooner *Bedwelty* out of Fowey. His children owned land as well as a fleet of seagoing vessels and were quite well-to-do.

A pretty and intelligent young woman, Susan was considered to be a catch for the right man of good family and property. The Tadds understandably wanted their daughter to choose a husband who could give her financial security and a comfortable life.

The year William Graham came to the Cornwall races, he arrived a few days early to let his horse rest and met Susan Tadd at the fair. It seems to have been love at first sight for both of them.

Susan's parents were horrified. The dashing Scot, they reminded her, was only a tenant farmer's son. And horse racing, as glamorous as it might seem, was no way to make a living. They forbade Susan to see William.

Even when William won the race, the Tadds refused to relent. Susan loved her family, but she loved William more. William was equally smitten with her. So he sold his horse and added the proceeds to his prize money to buy them both passage to Canada, where they could start their life as husband and wife. Susan never communicated with her parents again.

It was in the early 1870s that the newlyweds arrived in Toronto, a bustling provincial city on Lake

Ontario. Second only to Montreal in size, even then Toronto was the industrial and commercial center of Canada.

However, it was a difficult place for the young immigrants. William's skills as a horseman and farmer were not of much use in a city. The only work he could find was temporary and paid very little. When their first child was born, William felt even more frustrated by his inability to find a trade in this strange and, to him, unfriendly place.

Susan understood his unhappiness and will-ingly agreed to move to the country when she real-ized that there was a second baby on the way. William found a small farm to rent in Woodbridge, a village fourteen miles north of Toronto. As much as he hated working another man's land, as his father had done, William was much more comfortable in the country. At least he could feed his family.

The one concession to farming he could not make was to buy a workhorse. Horses on farms need to be strong, sturdy, and placid to plow and cart produce to market or hay to the barn. Like the peo-ple on farms, they work long hours. They have to withstand extremes in temperature, and they are not coddled in any way.

William's love of racehorses created a problem. He couldn't afford a horse good enough to train and win races. And he certainly couldn't pay for both a racehorse and a plowhorse. So he compromised by buying second-class thoroughbreds with the idea that he would breed them someday. In the meantime, the horses would have to work on the farm.

William's thoroughbreds were not very good at working the land, and they required extra care because they hadn't been bred for heavy labor. Susan sighed every time William came home with still another hopeless thoroughbred and tried to convince her of its potential. But she loved him and tried to be tolerant of his dream to get back into racing, a field in which he had proved he could succeed.

However, after Florence's birth, Susan found the Canadian winters difficult to withstand. No matter how she wrapped up, she always seemed to be cold. By the time Florence's younger sister Gladys was born, Susan had developed a cough that would sometimes keep the whole family awake through the night.

The new baby wore her out, and she found it difficult to regain her strength. Over her protests, William bundled Susan into a wagon and took her to a doctor in Toronto.

The doctor's diagnosis was tuberculosis, a frightening lung disease for which there was no treatment in the 1880s. He suggested that her only hope was to go to a sanatorium, where rest and fresh air might help her survive the illness.

Susan knew that was out of the question. They had no money for a sanatorium, and they had five small children to raise. On her return to the farm, she organized the household. Lillian and Christine were put in charge of housekeeping—cleaning, cooking, and mending. William was delegated to help his father with the farm work. Florence was put in charge of the horse which she loved. Baby Gladys wanted to go with Florence, but her mother was already upset about turning one daughter into a stableboy. Gladys was put in the care of Lillian and Christine.

Susan wanted to make sure that no one else in the family would develop her disease, which was believed to run in families. She was particularly concerned that her family stayed warm in bitter winter temperatures, and insisted that their shoes be insulated against the cold with layers of newspaper. Some fifty years later, Elizabeth Arden was still tucking neatly folded newspaper into her designer pumps on chilly days.

As her health declined, Susan began to think of her children's futures. She knew that William was a good father, but she also knew that he would never make enough money to give the children any of the advantages they might need to make a better life for themselves.

She knew that without an education, the young Grahams wouldn't be able to make any choices about their lives. That bothered Susan, and she decided to do something that would enable her children to receive an education.

She had never reconciled with her parents, and they had never forgiven her for disobeying them and eloping with William. But she had a wealthy Tadd aunt to whom she had been very close.

Without telling William, she wrote her aunt in Cornwall. She explained her situation and asked for help, not for herself or William, but for the children. She wanted money for their schooling, nothing more.

Her aunt agreed to the proposal, and Susan then told William what she had done. He was furious and humiliated that she had gone to the family that had disowned her. But when he saw how much it meant to her to know that her beloved children would have an education, he relented.

William promised Susan he would accept the money and use it only as she wished. He loved Susan and kept the promise.

Florence Nightingale Graham was six when her mother died. She did not understand why someone so good and so loving should be taken from her. She had adored her mother and then she lost her. She was to be wary of close relationships for the rest of her life.

At least the Graham children had each other. Florence continued to share horse care and horse dreams with her father. As she grew older, she accompanied him to market to sell his produce, and received her first lessons in selling. She also discovered she had a natural aptitude for it. Small for her age, she found that pretending to be younger than she was gave her an advantage. She could beguile the

women shoppers into buying almost anything from the farm—at whatever price she asked—when she presented herself as a very little girl.

What Florence didn't like was watching the housewives, better-dressed than she, haggle over prices with her father. She hated them for not paying the full price, which they could well afford. She was ashamed of her father for giving in to them.

Florence and her brother and sisters had plenty of chores, but they had fun, too. They couldn't afford to go into Toronto for amusement. Nor did they have a piano, the centerpiece of home entertainment in the late nineteenth century.

So the children made up their own games, and dreamed about the future. Lillian thought she might

At the turn of the century, trotting races were a popular attraction at small fairs across the United States and Canada.

like to be a painter. She enjoyed drawing and had a good eye for color. Christine, the homebody, wanted to get married and have a family of her own. Young William changed his mind a lot. Sometimes he thought it would be exciting to be a policeman. He once said he would like to be a "man about town," but his sisters didn't know what that was, and he couldn't explain it to them.

Florence always knew what she was going to be. "I want to be the richest little woman in the world," she told the others over and over again. What she couldn't tell them was how she was going to reach that goal. She didn't know herself.

Gladys always echoed what Florence said. She worshiped her sister and thought whatever Florence wanted to do would be fine for her, too.

Like other teenagers, the Graham girls loved to pour over magazines and catalogs and talk about music and dance and fashions in clothes. They turned part of the barn into their own private dance hall for practicing their own versions of the latest steps they had found out about at school.

When a French dance called the cancan became the rage, the Graham sisters used the barn to practice the high kicks it required. Never liking to be outdone, Florence kept practicing until she was sure she could kick higher than any of her sisters. She called them to watch, while she kicked a leg higher than before. Instead of triumph, she felt an agonizing pain.

She had thrown a hip out of joint. It was never to heal properly, and she would walk at a slight tilt all her life. Periodically, the joint would become inflamed and she would become bedridden, sometimes for months. But even when it happened, with all its inconvenience and pain, she never let it slow her down.

As a youngster Florence liked school. She was bright and curious and enjoyed learning. She hoped to go to college, something that more and more women were doing in the 1890s. It seemed an important step for a young female who wanted to be the richest woman in the world.

It was not to be. Florence's Tadd aunt died before she finished high school, and the money stopped. Her father told Florence she should attend a trade school so that she could learn to make a living and help support the family.

Florence was stunned with disappointment. She had no idea what kind of trade school she should go to because she didn't know what she wanted to do. She ran to the barn to be alone and think.

Patting one of the horses, she thought about all the times she had patted and massaged the sore ligaments and strained muscles of her father's horses. She had soothing hands, she knew. Didn't her family always come to her for help when they were in pain. She almost had a gift for healing.

Then she laughed. Wasn't her name Florence Nightingale Graham? She knew what she would do. She would go to nursing school and follow her namesake's profession.

The new occupation of telephone exchange operator was popular with women joining the work force for the first time.

Working Girl

*T*o enroll in nursing school, Florence had to go to Toronto. Her father was not too pleased about that. He had been unhappy and uncomfortable while there himself, and Florence was only a girl in her mid-teens.

He hated the idea of sending his daughter to the big city alone. But William Graham had no choice. There were no nursing schools in Woodbridge.

He was probably more frightened than Florence. Times were changing and for young people like Florence those changes were exciting. It was, after all, the 1890s.

Although most Americans and Canadians still lived on farms, new inventions that created new jobs were becoming part of ordinary life. The telephone, for example, had been patented the year before Florence was born. By the time she was ready to move to Toronto, more than 19,000 telephone operators were working in North America.

New businesses had brought about an avalanche of paperwork, which Philo Remington tried to resolve with his typewriting machine. The first models used only capital letters, but the year Florence was born, he brought out a shift-key version that would print out both capital and lower-case letters. By the time she moved to Toronto, there were more than 100,000 women working as typists in the United States and Canada.

As she bravely set off to make her way in the big city, she was not really alone. More than four million women were already in the work force in the United States. Their Canadian counterparts were not far behind.

More than a third of the working women at that time were domestic servants in other people's houses, cleaning and cooking. Another large group worked as waitresses or laundresses. But women were also making advances as artists, teachers, musicians, nurses, dressmakers, and tailors. Female bookkeepers, salespeople, and stenographers were becoming common.

Seventy percent of United States colleges had opened their doors to women by the 1890s. By the turn of the century, those colleges had graduated 7,000 women doctors, 3,000 women ministers, and 1,000 women lawyers. However, professional women—even those with advanced degrees—were not welcomed into established hospitals, churches, and law firms. They had to take their skills to small towns, where there weren't many trained men with degrees to compete with them.

But a beginning had been made. And Florence knew instinctively that she was a part of it.

She loved being in Toronto, where she could window-shop at the fanciest stores and watch the crowds at the popular restaurants.

She didn't, however, love nursing school. Her idealized picture of making people feel better with a soothing massage didn't materialize. Real life in a large hospital frightened and upset her. She found she didn't have the stomach for changing dressings or dealing with the unpleasant side of sickness.

It was during her nursing career that she met a biochemist who worked in the hospital laboratory. An intense young man, he was trying to develop a medicinal salve for treating skin blemishes.

Florence found the project fascinating, but not for the same reasons he did. Blessed with her mother's lovely English complexion, Florence had never worried about her skin. But many women were not so lucky. In that era, when many people contracted smallpox and other diseases that scarred their faces, women could do very little about bad skin. "Nice" women didn't wear makeup, and there were no effective skin preparations.

Florence saw the scientist's medicinal salve as a beauty cream. The more she thought about it, the better she liked the idea of a beauty cream. Let the other girls with the stronger stomachs take care of sick people in hospitals. She would make women happy by making them more beautiful.

She quit nursing school before the semester was up and returned to Woodbridge. William was not pleased that Florence had not finished out the course and gotten her money's worth.

"Don't worry, Papa," she said. "I am going to make us rich just as soon as I perfect my beauty cream."

Florence's idea was that she would sell her new product by mail. She was sure that as soon as women heard about a real beauty cream for the skin, the orders would roll in.

She may have been right. There were very few beauty preparations for women on the market. In the local pharmacy, they might buy glycerin and rosewater, a mild astringent, and a tin of talcum powder to keep them dry in warm weather.

For anything more exotic, women had to turn to ads in the popular magazines of the day or rummage through their favorite catalogs. The Sears Roebuck catalog, for example, carried so many diverse and wonderful items that it was known as the "wish book." Tucked between its furnishings for the house and fashions for the whole family, it offered such female beauty aids as combs, shell hairpins, curling irons, and perfumes.

But even the "wish book" was short on cosmetics. It sold cold cream, but most of its personal products for women were more patent medicines than beauty aids. Included were the World Famed Princess Tonic Hair Restorer and La Dore's Bust Food for "developing the bust and making it firm and round."

Florence enlisted the faithful Gladys as her helper and took over the Woodbridge kitchen as her laboratory. Each morning after breakfast, they would stoke up the big cast-iron stove with firewood and start melting down fats for the beauty cream. They experimented with various ingredients they felt would enhance their product.

The going was rougher than Florence had expected. Nothing came out the way she wanted. All the ingredients gave off terrible odors when they were heated. In fact, there were times when the whole family had to vacate the house for the afternoon to air it out.

Florence may have been discouraged, but she was hardly ready to give up—until the day the minister came to call. She met him at the door and invited him in. He looked at her sympathetically and handed her a basket of fresh eggs.

"My child," he said with real warmth. "You should never be too proud to ask for help." Florence was perplexed until he explained that neighbors had told him about her family's troubles. "No one should be reduced to eating rotten eggs, not in this community at least," he continued.

Florence finally realized what had happened. Neighbors had assumed that the terrible aroma coming from the Graham kitchen was the smell of rotten eggs cooking. They thought the family was too poor to eat anything else and had gone to the clergyman for help.

It was all Florence could do to keep a straight face while she thanked the minister and ushered him out the front door. As soon as he was gone, she raced to the kitchen to share the joke with Gladys. The girls laughed until tears rolled down their cheeks.

Unfortunately, William did not think the incident funny.

"That does it, Florence!" he cried. "You have two choices—you can get married or you can go to Toronto and get an honest job."

Florence had never considered getting married. She was a pretty, lively girl who had certainly attracted the attention of young men at school and later in Toronto. She had never encouraged any of them, however. She really did want to be the richest little woman in the world. And, although she wasn't sure how she was going to amass her wealth, she seemed to know that she had to do it herself.

Also, as much as she loved her father, she did not want to live as grim a life as her mother had. Her mother, Florence believed, had lost everything in marriage—her family, her financial security, and, finally, her life.

So Florence returned to Toronto to join the new tide of independent working girls. She didn't have a trade, nor, in fact, a complete education. But she was not afraid of the long hours offices required, and she was eager to learn all she could.

Her first job was not very glamorous. She became the receptionist for a manufacturing company that made trusses and athletic supports for men. In the beginning, she didn't mind. She was too thrilled about living on her own, making her own money, and having all of Toronto for her entertainment and pleasure. She met other young people to explore the city with on Sundays, her only day off.

✳

"You have two choices—you can get married or you can go to Toronto and get an honest job."

Eventually she found a better job as a teller in a bank. Always on the lookout for opportunities that would pay more money, Florence then took a job with a real-estate office as a secretary. She was presented with a sturdy Remington shift-key typewriter to speed up her paperwork, the very machine that had been perfected the year of her birth. But she had overestimated her mechanical abilities.

The machine required dexterity she didn't have and seemed to have a mind of its own. She never learned to use it and was fired. It was the first and last time she was ever to lose a job. Many years later, with a staff of typists at her disposal, she still insisted on writing her letters by hand.

Florence slowly made her way from job to job in Toronto. As the years rolled by, she continued to work hard and enjoy the city, but still she was looking for something that was eluding her. Her brother moved to New York City, because he felt there was more opportunity in the United States. Christine, true to her ambitions, got married and started a family.

Lillian put her artistic skills to work for a milliner. Ladies' hats were at their most extravagant at the turn of the century. Women did not appear in public without them. They were elaborate creations with poufs of lace, yards of ribbons, whole bouquets of flowers, egret and ostrich feathers. Nests of birds even festooned some of the most fashionable bonnets.

Gladys couldn't make up her mind among her beaux, but it seemed clear that marriage was in her future. Only Florence appeared to be drifting.

Toronto was bustling. Automobiles were becoming more commonplace. The first silent-movie theaters appeared. Called nickelodeons because they cost a nickel for an evening's entertainment, they offered comedies and dramas and a view of life in other places. Between reels, notices to the audience were projected on the screen. "Ladies without escorts are cordially invited," one read. "A baby is crying. Could it be yours?" said another. Florence loved going to the nickelodeon. She went as often as the bill changed.

In 1907 Florence changed jobs again. She went to work for a dentist for a higher salary than she had ever had before. She worked as his receptionist, his assistant, and his bookkeeper. While going over his accounts, she realized that the job wasn't going to last very long if she didn't do something to help.

The poor man wasn't bringing in enough money to cover rent, supplies, and her salary and still allow him to support his family. Florence didn't want to lose this job, so she composed a letter to his patients, suggesting that if they didn't come in for an immediate checkup they were in peril of losing their teeth. She also intimated that neglecting their teeth would ultimately cause them extreme pain.

To her great relief, the dentist's business doubled within the year. She didn't realize that her talent for marketing a product was developing.

She had saved her job, but she was still restless. She was almost thirty—middle-aged, in her view—and none of her dreams seemed to be on the horizon. Most women her age in the first decade of the twentieth century had long ago settled down with families or careers. Florence wasn't ready to settle for anything yet.

She knew she was in a rut. And she knew she had the energy and drive to make something important happen. She thought about her brother in New York. Willie was doing well in business there and always said that there was more opportunity in the United States. Maybe he was right.

Florence made up her mind to go to New York. She went to Woodbridge first to tell her father. William Graham wasn't really happy about her living alone in Toronto. New York was out of the question. He forbade her to go, but he must have known it wouldn't stop her.

To William, Florence was still a young girl, not a woman embarking on her thirties. Florence still looked twenty. She was not quite five feet two inches tall. She had fine auburn hair, sparkling blue eyes, and a fair, clear skin with good color. She had the hourglass figure much admired in the early 1900s. Her slim ankles and well-shaped feet would serve her well when skirts got shorter. Only her hands detracted from her essentially graceful appearance. They were short-fingered and strong. They might have worried her when she looked in a mirror then, but they would prove to be one of her greatest assets.

Florence herself did not feel thirty as she set off for New York. She was filled with the hope and expectation of a twenty-year-old. Perhaps she was so disappointed with her Toronto experience that she just decided to relive the decade in another place. Whatever the reason, she forever after would claim that she was in her twenties when she pulled off her early successes in New York.

Big Dreams in the Big City

When Florence Nightingale Graham stepped off of the train that had brought her to New York's Grand Central Station, she joined the largest wave of immigration the United States would ever experience.

Like the half a million other immigrants pouring into the country each year, she came to make a new and better life. But she had advantages. First of all, she spoke English. The great majority of immigrants at that time were from Eastern Europe and Italy. Language was a serious barrier for them because if they didn't speak English, they couldn't get a good job.

Florence also had an education. She had come close to finishing high school, and she had learned a number of skills in her Toronto jobs. By her own admission, she was a whiz at bookkeeping and she had, on occasion, shown a flair for selling and public relations.

Big Dreams in the Big City

Also, she had spent more than a dozen years in a bustling provincial city, not too different from many American cities in the Midwest. New York, a sophisticated port city, held exciting surprises for her, but she did not experience the culture shock that affected so many other immigrants. She already read American magazines, was thrilled by American silent movies, and followed American fashion.

Her response to New York was love at first sight. Far from being intimidated by the sight of such early skyscrapers as the Flatiron and Singer buildings, she marveled at them. The Manhattan Bridge—the second breathtaking span over the East River to Brooklyn—had just been opened for traffic. The first gas-powered taxi cab had appeared on New York's streets only two years earlier, and already the number of horse-drawn hansom cabs was declining drastically. Traffic from automobiles, mixed with horse-drawn vans, was noisy and confusing. The post office had just introduced its first mail-delivery truck, and the fire department was about to try its first motorized fire engine.

But the most remarkable form of transportation was the sparkling new underground train system. Florence found a room in a modest but decent house on 94th Street near Riverside Drive, a lovely residential neighborhood where she could look out over the Hudson River. With the business part of the city still concentrated below 50th Street, Florence quickly learned to make her way around Manhattan.

She wanted to see everything. Galleries, museums, department stores like Wanamaker's and Bonwit Teller's, restaurants like Sherry's and Delmonico's, theaters, and nickelodeon houses were all on her itinerary. She carefully studied the fashionable women she encountered in each of these places, and returned to her room to take out needle and thread and update her own wardrobe.

Though she was in touch with her brother William, who was beginning to make money with his

business deals in the city, she made it clear that she was in New York to carve out her own life. She had not come to be taken under his wing.

She quickly found a job as a bookkeeper for E.R. Squibb and Sons, one of the leading American chemical and pharmaceutical companies. Just as the hospital laboratory where she did her nurse's training had captured her imagination, the spanking-clean, modern workrooms for chemists at Squibb's drew her attention.

Her interest in creating a real beauty cream was still very much with her. She befriended several of the Squibb scientists and bombarded them with questions. Obviously, her idea about selling this kind of product had not disappeared with the bad odors in the Woodbridge kitchen. The chemists did not share her interest in producing such a cream, however. They felt they had much more important medical projects to pursue.

In her explorations of New York, Florence discovered several women already addressing the problem of female skin care. Calling themselves "beauty culturists," these entrepreneurs had small establishments where they massaged their preparations into their clients' faces. They claimed to be able to rejuvenate youthful complexions scientifically.

Florence was fascinated. Although these practitioners referred to their shops as beauty parlors, these establishments were not like the traditional hair salons where women went to get their hair washed and curled. The first beauty parlors or hairdressing salons dated from the late 1860s (the first one opened in Philadelphia). These salons were popular for two reasons. First, hair styles were changing and becoming more elaborate. It was difficult for a woman herself to pile and pin her tresses artfully over a "rat" and create the bouffant style popular then. And, second, these shops were a comfortable place for women to meet and share gossip. Going to their hairdresser was a pleasant break in the day for homebound housewives.

Skin-care salons made a lot of sense to Florence, and she was determined to find out more about them. The one that she decided was the most interesting was run by an Irish woman, Mrs. Eleanor Adair, who had started similar establishments in Paris and London.

Mrs. Adair advertised her treatments in ladies' magazines. Her new facial method included what she called "Ganesh muscle strapping" plus the application of "Ganesh Diable" skin tonic, muscle oil, cream, and "other astonishing Ganesh beauty aids." Her ads referred to "wonderfully magnetic hands" that would pat in the preparations. Treatments cost $2.50 each.

Mrs. Adair was not trying to appeal to the new working woman, who earned about $12 or $13 a week and probably could not have afforded such an extravagance. She was after wealthy matrons who worried about their looks and had the leisure time and money to do something about them.

Florence wanted to get her foot in the door of Mrs. Adair's skin-treatment parlor and find out what these Ganesh products were. The first job open there was that of cashier, the lowest-paying one on the payroll. Florence took it.

She never did find out what "Ganesh" meant, but she saw that the muscle strapping involved taping the chin and lower jaw to the rest of the head before the tonics and creams were massaged into the face. And she also saw that the clients' skin did have a becoming glow when the treatments were completed.

Florence begged Mrs. Adair to train her to do the treatments. Mrs. Adair ran a tight operation. She only agreed to teach Florence her techniques if Florence understood that she would receive no extra money for it. And Florence still had to cover her cashiering duties. For once, something was more important to Florence than money. She accepted the terms and became a quick and willing apprentice.

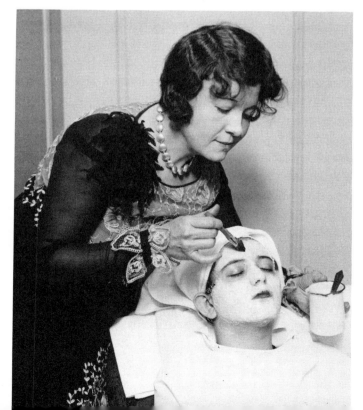

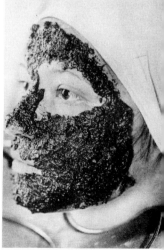

Early skin treatments included a paraffin, or "kaloric," mask (left) and masks of vegetable compounds. Both were thought to stimulate circulation and soften the skin.

It was not long before customers were asking if the "nice Canadian" could do their treatments. Florence—delighted with the response—was pleased to be singled out. Her strong square hands were adept at massage. They may not have been "magnetic," as Mrs. Adair's ads said, but they felt assured and capable in the new work. She did have a special touch with them, she discovered. And she began to suspect that the success of the treatments depended more on the massage and patting than on the products she was working into her customers' faces.

In fact, she realized that Mrs. Adair's secret beauty formulas left a lot to be desired. They didn't reek like the potions she had tried to make in Woodbridge, but they didn't smell particularly good either. And they felt greasy.

Florence soon became popular enough to ask for and receive a raise. It was a turning point for her. She loved her work and felt she was finally doing something for which she had an instinct. She was making enough money to send some to her family, and she was at last exploring a field in which she felt at home.

She had very little time to worry about a social life. In addition to her job at Eleanor Adair's, she had advertised her services as a manicurist. She saw customers at home in the evenings. Here again her capable hands allowed her to work adroitly. Plus, she was learning about another aspect of beauty care.

Florence analyzed every part of Mrs. Adair's operation. She saw that the Adair advertisements seemed to be successful because they appealed to a kind of snobbishness. They boasted of clients in Paris and London who were royalty and gentlewomen of the highest rank.

Florence didn't really believe the advertising, but she could understand its appeal in a city like New York, where new fortunes were being made every day and where social standing had more to do with money than family background. Women whose husbands had recently struck it rich often needed help in learning how to dress appropriately and how to do their hair for their new social lives. Beauty was prized in these new circles, and Florence was aware of this.

Social-climbing women wanted to look their best as they entered more elite realms. Florence herself was not a little awed by the wealthy grande dames of New York who entertained lavishly and were described in the newspapers attending opening nights and parties in extravagantly expensive gowns and jewelry.

Florence also thought about the name of Mrs. Adair's products. Ganesh was not a real word, although it might have been a variation on *ganache*, the French word for lower jaw. That didn't seem very glamorous to Florence. But she did understand that the name was supposed to make people think of exotic sources of beauty expertise.

She thought she could do better in naming beauty products if she ever had any of her own to sell. She knew they would have to feel better and smell better than Mrs. Adair's. Florence spent more and more time thinking about how she would run her own beauty-culture parlor.

Her dream was beginning to take a definite shape. She no longer wanted to sell her beauty cream by mail. She liked the idea of having a place where women would come to her for treatment.

Working at Mrs. Adair's, she discovered that she was a good saleswoman, even among a sophisticated, wealthy group of women. Her soft voice and clipped Canadian speech appealed to these clients, since it sounded slightly British. The new American rich, a little self-conscious about their poor and often uneducated ancestors, tended to believe that the English were much more cultured and refined than they were. Florence benefited from this belief.

She enjoyed the company of these women. While she might not be the richest woman in the world, she at least could spend her time working

The Cornelius Vanderbilt Mansion on Fifth Avenue and 58th Street was based on a French chateau. Now the site is occupied by the Bergdorf Goodman department store.

around rich women, advising them on their beauty care, and soaking up their gossip about a world that sounded quite wonderful to a young woman who had grown up on a tenant farm outside Toronto.

Florence was becoming a workaholic, but a happy one. She was never to change. Like other working women of her day, she was expected to be on the job ten hours a day, six days a week. She gave manicures in the evenings after supper, and on her day off she tried to keep up with exciting new developments in her adopted city.

One of her favorite outings was to walk up Fifth Avenue, starting at 42nd Street right above the

Croton reservoir, where the city got its water. As she headed north, she would pass Sherry's on the left and Delmonico's on the right, two favorite dining spots for the fashionable people who lived along her most treasured avenue.

This upper part of Fifth Avenue was known as New York's Gold Coast because it was lined with mansions, many of which architecturally resembled châteaux from France and castles from the Rhine Valley in Germany. These dwellings of the very rich were exuberant expressions of new money. What they lacked in authenticity and artistic design, they made up for in size and expensive decoration.

Florence loved these mansions and memorized the names engraved on their brass door plaques. There were four Vanderbilt mansions before 59th Street. Frick, Gould, Sage, Goelet, Morton, Brice, she would say to herself as she passed each of the urban palaces. John Jacob Astor, the fur baron, lived in the sixties. Havemeyer, Thaw, Bostwick, Harriman, Thorne, Pell, Harkness, Whitney, and Brokaw were more magical names to remember. Next came Dana, Phipps, Lewis, and, finally, at the corner of 92nd Street, was the house of Andrew Carnegie, the steel magnate. Florence would be exhausted, but exhilarated with her tour of Manhattan real estate.

She thrived on the sense of possibilities the city seemed to offer. She was getting a feeling for what she really wanted to do; she was learning everything she could about this new business of beauty; and she knew she would be ready when the right opportunity came along.

In the small world of beauty culturists in New York, she was earning a reputation for good technique as a facial masseuse and for even better technique as a saleswoman. Her colleagues found her talents quite amazing for a young woman in her early twenties.

Florence didn't have the heart to tell them they were mistaken about her age. If she looked twenty, well, that wasn't her fault. And, really, was her age anybody's business but her own?

To anyone else, Florence's life would have seemed dreary. She worked day and night; she had barely any time to herself; and, when she did have a holiday, she had no one to share it with. But she was happy. She knew she was biding her time until the right opportunity came along. And she knew it would.

What's in a Name?

*O*nce she was sure what she wanted to do—have her own beauty-culture studio—Florence became an untiring researcher into the business. Even while she worked for Eleanor Adair, she often visited rival establishments on her lunch hour.

She wanted to try out competitors' products and see if they had useful application methods that she might adapt for her own use. She also wanted to check out their selling techniques and how they decorated their treatment rooms.

With her youthful looks and flawless complexion, she must have appeared to be an odd client.

In the course of her research, Florence discovered a line of beauty creams and tonics that she thought to be much superior to Mrs. Adair's. They were the creation of a woman named Mrs. Elizabeth Hubbard.

Mrs. Hubbard, like Florence, had ambition. She also had the one thing Florence had never been able to come up with by herself—acceptable beauty products.

On the other hand, Florence had talents that Mrs. Hubbard badly needed. She had skilled hands for applying beauty products, and she had a flair for selling to a clientele who could afford to pay dearly for the dream of beauty.

Selling beauty products to women was a bit tricky in the early part of the twentieth century. It was not considered proper to help nature along in normal society. Makeup—lipstick, rouge, face powder, and eye shadow—was acceptable only in the theater. Most actresses were still not considered a part of decent society. Many were assumed to be "loose" women with no morals. They may have been visited by wealthy men, but they were rarely invited into proper people's houses.

However, the ideal of beauty in that era was set by such stars of the stage as Maxine Elliott (the painter James McNeill Whistler called her the "girl with the midnight eyes"), Julia Marlowe (best known for the role of Juliet in Shakespeare's *Romeo and Juliet*), Ethel Barrymore (the serene, throaty-voiced princess of America's theatrical royal family), and Maude Adams, who captured the hearts of all Americans as Peter Pan.

To sell beauty treatments to society clients who wanted to look as lovely as these actresses, but who felt morally superior, required a delicate approach. Florence seemed to suggest just the right mixture of serious concern for healthy skin care and promise of eternal youth to pull it off.

Florence and Mrs. Hubbard each saw the benefits of joining forces. Mrs. Hubbard, probably ignorant of Florence's real age, considered herself to be the senior partner.

However, she deferred to Florence on such marketing issues as where they would be located and what kind of clients they would try to attract. Florence wanted to cater to the kind of wealthy, socially prominent women that Mrs. Adair was serving.

One way to do that, she believed, was to set up shop in a fashionable spot that would be convenient for these women, many of whom lived on upper Fifth Avenue and shopped at department stores on lower Fifth Avenue. She and Mrs. Hubbard looked right in the middle near Sherry's, where their prospective customers often lunched.

Florence found them a space, the third floor of 509 Fifth Avenue. The building was between 42nd Street and 43rd Street, a few doors down from Delmonico's and directly across the street from Sherry's. A lovely brownstone, the building was just what Florence thought appropriate for the rich, relaxed atmosphere she wanted to create for the business.

There were problems. They actually didn't need the whole third floor right away and the rent was $75 a month, more than Florence ever made at Mrs. Adair's. Florence was surprised that Mrs. Hubbard didn't make more of a fuss about the rent. She was prepared to argue about what must have seemed a terrible extravagance, but she never had to. Mrs. Hubbard must have known how important the location was for the firm.

Florence had other novel ideas. She wanted to call their establishment a beauty *salon* instead of a *parlor*. To her this sounded more gracious and maybe even evoked an image of a Parisian drawing room. Parlor, she thought, suggested the front rooms of dingy boardinghouses or, even worse, a hairdresser's place. Mrs. Hubbard agreed to call it a salon.

But she was not as easily convinced about Florence's ideas for naming her products. Florence had always hated Mrs. Adair's choice of "Ganesh" for her line. It was a harsh word, and it didn't mean anything to anyone. Florence believed that the name should suggest exotic origins, but she also felt that it could do more. A name should also evoke images of beauty.

Florence wanted to call the products "Grecian." It made her think of beautiful classic statues like the Venus de Milo, sunlit white buildings, and brilliant seas. Mrs. Hubbard said it made her think of ruins, and reminded Florence that the Venus de Milo had no arms.

Florence thought Mrs. Hubbard had no imagination. She may have been right, because Mrs. Hubbard couldn't come up with a better name. The products were called Grecian by default.

Mrs. Hubbard didn't need imagination to insist that the name of their firm be Mrs. Elizabeth Hubbard. She felt entitled because the products they were selling were hers. She also pointed out to Florence that if they called themselves Hubbard and Graham, people would think they were lawyers or accountants. Florence agreed with that, but she thought they might use both their first names.

"Mrs. Elizabeth Hubbard and Miss Florence Nightingale Graham" was just too long, Mrs. Hubbard said. And, she pointed out, the name Florence Nightingale would make people think of hospitals and sickness, not beauty and youth.

Florence, who had spent a long time honing her ideas for a beauty salon, wasn't about to give up her dream just when she was on the brink of making it come true. But she must have had some serious second thoughts about her stubborn new partner.

Florence, in her own way, was just as stubborn. And she knew how to bide her time. So, swallowing her pride, she gave in and accepted her partner's name for the business.

Neither of the partners had much money to put into their establishment, but both agreed that it should be as well appointed as they could afford to make it. That meant papering the walls, putting a good carpet, upholstered chairs, and fine draperies in the reception room, and making the treatment rooms spotless.

It also meant hiring an expensive sign painter to letter Mrs. Hubbard's name in gold leaf on the window that faced out on Fifth Avenue.

They announced their new business by taking an ad in *Vogue* magazine, even then one of the most prestigious periodicals for women. Reading like an announcement, the copy said that Mrs. Elizabeth Hubbard had opened a new salon at 509 Fifth Avenue to serve "women socially prominent in the Metropolis and suburbs." It mentioned her famous Grecian skin tonic, muscle creams, and oils as well as a new method of face treatments. The price for the facials was given as $2 each or six for $10.

Florence, who had written the ad, had purposely undercut Mrs. Adair's prices. That way she hoped to attract some of her former clients. She fully intended to raise the prices in the near future. It was her belief then—and she held it throughout her career—that people valued a product more if they had to pay dearly for it.

The only thing new about Florence's method of face treatments was the product that she worked into the skin. She continued to use the strapping and massaging that she had learned from Mrs. Adair.

Clients easily found their way to the new salon. Florence acted as treatment woman and Mrs. Hubbard busied herself in the back room with batches of cream, oil, and tonic. This separation of duties kept the partners out of each other's way and made their uneasy alliance seem workable at first.

When the rent came due, Mrs. Hubbard handed the statement for the second $75 payment to Florence. "That will have to come out of your tip money," she announced.

Florence was flabbergasted. "That was never part of the deal!" she protested.

"I make the product. You pay the rent," replied Mrs. Hubbard.

❋

It was her belief that people valued a product more if they had to pay dearly for it.

Florence was livid. Also, she didn't make as much as $75 a month in tips yet, so the proposition was all the more infuriating.

Florence was not afraid to defend herself. She told Mrs. Hubbard that her contribution to the salon was a skill for massage that was much more beneficial to women's faces than any cream. Actually, many years later, dermatologists would confirm that.

However, Mrs. Hubbard was not convinced. The women argued late into the night and settled nothing. They each stormed home to make a decision.

Their choices were indicative of their futures. Each arose early the next morning, determined to take action on the problem. Mrs. Hubbard went to see her lawyer. Florence, much more shrewdly, went first to the bank to withdraw $75 and then to the landlord of 509 Fifth Avenue. Mrs. Hubbard received advice on dissolving a partnership. Florence received the lease for the salon in her own name.

Within the month, Mrs. Elizabeth Hubbard announced a move to new quarters at 505 Fifth Avenue, two doors south of her former address.

Florence always felt she still had the better location because women who lived on upper Fifth Avenue would pass her salon first.

Happy as she might have been to be rid of her disagreeable partner and have exclusive rights to the new salon, Florence did have more than a few problems to face. What should she call her salon? Where would she get the money to buy or make her own beauty products? How would she finance more advertising to announce her own business? What about new furnishings to replace what Mrs. Hubbard had taken with her?

First, she thought about names. She loved her own name, Florence Nightingale Graham. But Florence Nightingale herself had died recently. The papers were full of tributes and eulogies, and Florence thought it would not be appropriate to name a beauty salon for her. It would be misunderstood.

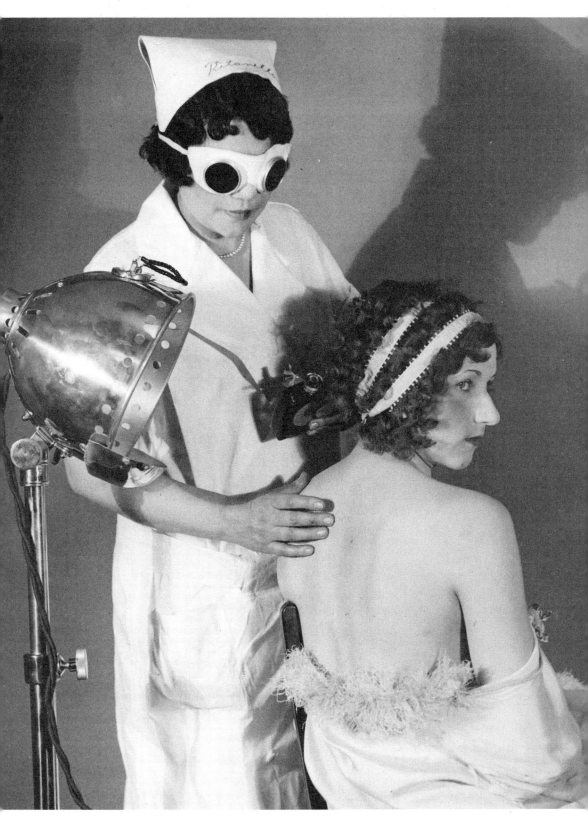

The first decades of the twentieth century saw the introduction of numerous beauty treatments. Here a nurse demonstrates the "Keene Violet Sun Ray Machine" to a customer.

The name Florence Graham seemed too prosaic. Florence Tadd Graham was not very different. Well, she thought, if I can't use my own name, I at least want one that sounds like the kind of person I want to be.

Musing over the name problem in the salon, she looked at the expensive gold leaf lettering on her window. It looked so pretty with its curlicues. Where would she ever get the money to have it redone, she wondered.

Then, it hit her. She might not need to have the whole name painted over. What if she kept the Elizabeth? That was really a lovely name. Elizabeth Graham? Elizabeth Tadd? She wasn't sure about the last name, but she felt good enough about using the name Elizabeth to go home for the night.

After dinner, she went over her accounts. She was getting a clear picture of what she had to do and how much money it would take to do it.

She decided to take a break and think about something else before she went to sleep. She had a volume of poems by the English poet Alfred Tennyson beside her bed, a volume she had first read in high school. Leafing through the book, she stopped at a poem called *Enoch Arden*, which had been a favorite of hers since her school days. She said the title aloud and thought it had a lovely resonance.

And then, of course, she tried it with Elizabeth. Elizabeth Arden. Yes, she liked the sound. But she wasn't completely convinced. She got out of bed and went to her desk. "Good luck!" she wrote in large letters across a piece of note paper. She folded the paper and put it in a matching envelope. She carefully addressed the envelope in her best handwriting: "Mrs. Elizabeth Arden, 509 Fifth Avenue, Third Floor, New York, New York " and mailed it.

Even with horse-drawn vans, the United States Mail was pretty efficient in 1910. When Florence went through the morning mail the next day in the salon, the note addressed to Elizabeth Arden was there. It looked just right to her. She had a new name. She sent a note to the sign painter that very day.

Coming to work in the mornings, she got a great boost just looking up at the third-floor window. "Mrs. Elizabeth Arden," it read on the first line. "Beauty Culture," said a second line. "By appointment only," said the last line.

Florence, now Elizabeth, had retained the Mrs. from Mrs. Hubbard's sign not just to save money. She felt that a Mrs. carried more authority than a Miss. And she felt she needed authority to run a successful business and attract the customers she wanted. Eventually she would drop the Mrs. when she felt confident enough to get away with it.

Women were still second-class citizens in the United States in 1910. They could not vote in political elections. In many states they could not own property. In even more states, if they were married, they had no claims on money they earned themselves. In most states they did not have equal rights of guardianship over their own children.

Elizabeth Arden was not then a suffragette because she was too busy working on her own economic freedom to worry about whether she could vote or not. From her practical perspective, her independence was completely dependent on how much money she could make and bank by herself. With money, she believed, she could buy whatever it was she needed. She was too impatient to wait for laws to help her, and she was not interested in the status of other women.

Mrs. Elizabeth Arden *did* sound respectable and lilting. But even with her satisfying new name, Florence was still facing some challenges that she would soon have to solve. Florence's savings were running out, and the rent remained $75 a month.

As Elizabeth Arden, Florence was ready to take some bold new initiatives. As Florence Nightingale Graham, she continued to give manicures at night in her room.

Elizabeth Arden's salons inspired many women to enter the beauty business; lessons in manicuring and haircutting were included in high school hygiene classes such as this one.

Imagination, Daring . . . and Work, Work, Work

*P*leased with her new professional name, Florence began to think of herself as Elizabeth Arden. This new and dynamic person seemed to have inexhaustible energy and imagination. It was she who always had an answer for whatever difficulty Florence thought might kill the business before it ever opened.

Elizabeth Arden, for example, was capable of creating new skin preparations in the back room of her salon. Florence had watched Mrs. Hubbard stir up her creams and tonics in their makeshift laboratory. But she was still sensitive to her awful-smelling experiments at home. Florence by herself was wary of cooking up her own products.

But as Elizabeth Arden, she seemed to gain a kind of self-confidence about her abilities. She had, after all, spent a lot of time discussing skin creams with scientists. She knew more about what went into a good product than most people.

One thing she was very sure about. Although Mrs. Hubbard's concoctions were an improvement over Mrs. Adair's, even they were not very pleasant-smelling. In each batch, she began to include larger quantities of the best fragrances she could buy. It cost more to make her facial preparations that way, but Elizabeth Arden didn't believe in cutting corners.

She planned to charge high prices for her services because she was advertising them as the best. She wanted to make sure they really were the best. If it took more expensive ingredients to make a more appealing product, she was willing to spend the money.

And so Elizabeth Arden created her own line of beauty products. They felt good and they smelled good and she was very proud of them. Now she could turn her energies to other matters.

No longer having to argue with Mrs. Hubbard over every decision, she was free to create the salon of her dreams. She wanted it to be luxurious and restful. Coming to her salon should be a treat, not a chore. She wanted women to look forward to their beauty treatments.

Florence Graham, still giving manicures at night, was anxious to get the salon opened so that it could begin making money. She worried about where the capital would come from to refurbish the space and pay the women she would have to hire to give the treatments. She decided to try out her new confidence on her brother William.

He laughed at the idea that she had to change her name to open a new business. He saw nothing wrong with Graham, which was an honest and respectable family name. But he also found that his sister in her new identity had become a persuasive saleswoman.

He didn't really understand the business she was trying to get started. He felt that he appreciated beautiful women as much as any man, but he certainly wasn't interested in how they got that way.

However, he had just made a tidy profit on one of his investments, and he decided to help his little sister out. He really didn't care what she did with the money. He saw it as a nice family gesture, and he was sure he would never see a penny of it again.

Elizabeth Arden would be known all her life as an extravagant woman who spent money recklessly. It was an effective pose. Florence Graham had described herself years before as a "whiz of a book-keeper," and she always knew how to balance an account. For her new business, she knew she had to spend money in order to make money.

When Elizabeth Arden asked her brother for $6,000 to launch her salon, she knew exactly how she would spend every penny. In 1910 the average worker was lucky to bring in $700 a year. The $6,000 Elizabeth wanted was a princely sum. Her brother was shocked at the amount, but he gamely made out a check to Mrs. Elizabeth Arden for $6,000.

Elizabeth lost no time in putting her capital to work. First, she invested in the ingredients for making larger batches of her new sweet-smelling creams and tonics.

Later in her career she would take months and months to pick out appropriate names for new products. The most she hoped to accomplish with a name for this first line was to confuse Mrs. Adair's and Mrs. Hubbard's customers. She wanted to get them into her salon. If her products sounded like theirs, their clients might come into her beauty-culture establishment by mistake. Once she had them inside, she was sure she could keep them.

From Mrs. Adair's Ganesh, she had created Mrs. Hubbard's Grecian products. It was a short slip of the tongue to Elizabeth Arden's Venetian preparations.

She carried the Venetian theme into her decor. Venice, Italy, is an ancient and beautiful port city on the Adriatic Sea. Built on a series of islands, its streets are canals and waterways. Transportation is by boat, rather than automobile, and its taxis are the famous gondolas with their graceful high prows. Venice is also famous for its delicate glass products.

Elizabeth invested in a Venetian glass chandelier for her reception room. To continue the theme, she decided to display samples of her products among Venetian glass objects in glass cases along the walls of the same room.

She bought an Oriental carpet for the floor and graceful French antique chairs. For the walls, she chose pink damask fabric and a deeper pink edging of braided satin ribbon. She was very happy with the pink. It reflected flattering light on the room and the people in it.

She used the same pink in the three treatment cubicles, which looked like tidy little powder rooms. They had mirrors and special chairs to keep the clients comfortable while she strapped their chins and massaged their faces.

While Elizabeth created a rich and comfortable ambiance in her salon with fine antiques, she was not opposed to new technology. She had her chandelier wired for electricity. No odorous gas lamps would light her salon.

The workroom where she created her beauty products was left plain and businesslike. It was not for clients to see. That left one last room to deal with in her rented space. It was a large room and she couldn't afford to furnish it.

She decided that the smart thing to do would be to sublet that room to someone else. Then it would at least be paying for itself until she had enough business to justify its cost. But she needed a tenant.

Elizabeth, the businesswoman, came up with her own solution. She decided to rent it to someone whose business would be an extension of her own. They could then refer clients back and forth, and both establishments would profit from the arrangement.

Considering the New York beauty business people she knew, Elizabeth found just the right tenants.

Two sisters, Jessica and Clara Ogilvie, who had recently opened a tiny hair salon on 34th Street, had developed a series of products for hair and scalp treatments that Elizabeth believed to be superior to others on the market.

In fact, Elizabeth had been among their first customers because her own hair was fine-textured and difficult to manage. She liked their approach to hair care. It was much like her approach to skin care. They used their products to promote a healthy scalp, which in turn enhanced the natural shine and beauty of the hair.

The Ogilvie sisters also had an agreement with another sister who was a fashionable milliner. She would suggest to her clients that their new hats might look more becoming on a new hairdo. She would then recommend that they visit her sisters' salon. Jessica and Clara would, for their part, encourage their patrons to top off new hairdos with a splendid new bonnet from Gladys Ogilvie's shop.

Gladys had a wealthy clientele. Her hats started at $45 and then went up in price. Working women who made $12 a week could not afford to spend almost a month's salary on a new bonnet.

Elizabeth set about convincing the Ogilvie sisters that her location on Fifth Avenue would be to their benefit. The city was moving uptown, she told them, and they had better move up, too. Their current shop was around the corner from the very posh Waldorf Astoria Hotel, then located at Fifth Avenue and 34th Street (the Empire State Building now stands on that spot), and the sisters were hesitant to make a change.

Elizabeth had another selling point. Their rent would be less if they moved in with her. Since they were just starting out, that did make a difference to them.

Elizabeth also got them excited about the idea of their referring clients to each other. It made sense to them that a woman who was concerned about her

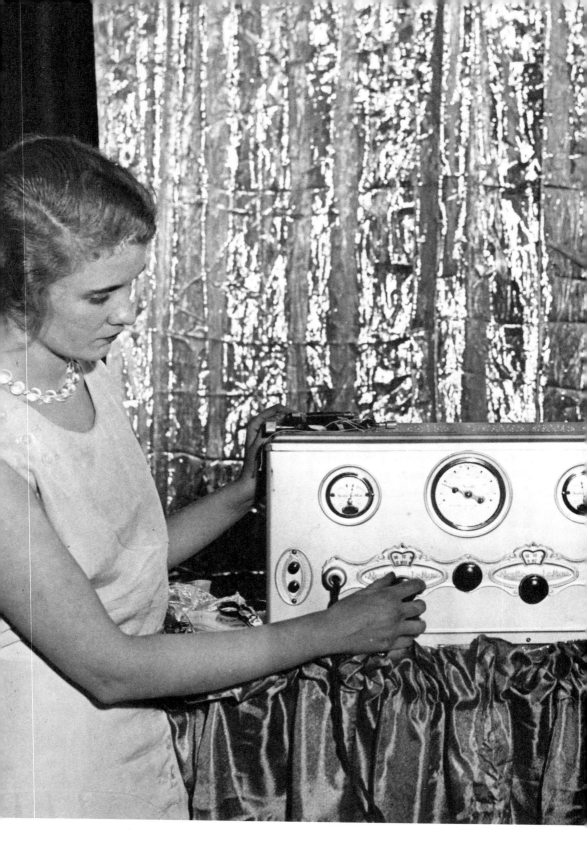

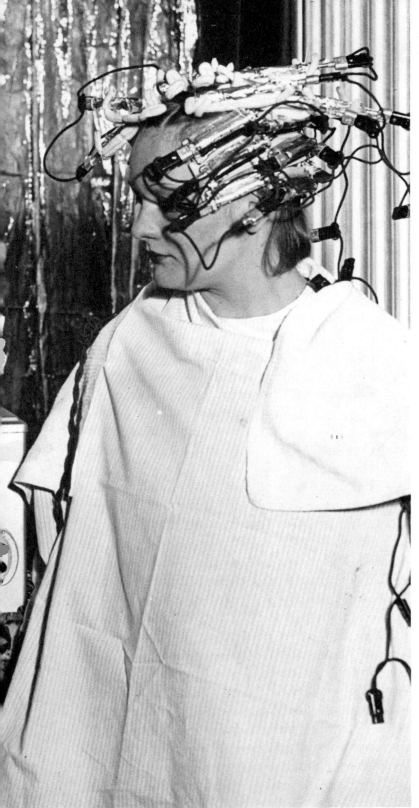

*As permanent waves
became more common, the
equipment for creating
them was refined. An
earlier machine was
powered by wires that
were suspended over the
customer's head.*

skin would also care about how her hair looked. And, as Elizabeth kept reminding them, what would make a hat look better than a glowing complexion?

Jessica and Clara Ogilvie had one last concern. They knew Elizabeth Arden was creating her own beauty products, just as they were developing their own hair products. They made Elizabeth sign an agreement not to sell any shampoo or hair tonics. Since she had developed neither, she graciously conceded.

The Ogilvie sisters moved into 509 Fifth Avenue during their first year of business. Whether this was a crucial move on their part or not, no one will ever know. But they were to become quite wealthy and famous for their hair products.

The Ogilvies would always say that watching Elizabeth Arden build her business was an astonishing phenomenon. They were in awe of their landlord's ability to sell. And they were equally impressed with the way she trained her treatment women to sell. They may have picked up a few pointers themselves.

To open her business, Elizabeth felt she needed three employees. Two would join her in giving treatments and a third would act as receptionist and office manager. She would create the products and do the books herself after hours. Of course, part of her leisure time was still taken up with giving manicures, but somehow she knew she would be able to manage.

One of the first people she hired was a young woman named Irene Delaney, who was her first receptionist. As the business grew and Elizabeth Arden grew more powerful and autocratic in her management, she would be known as a difficult person for whom to work. Many people joined and left the company very quickly, but Irene Delaney worked for Elizabeth Arden for forty years.

Elizabeth, always practical and hardworking, put her brother's money into the things she thought would distinguish her beauty salon from everyone else's. She believed that spending a great deal of money for good furniture and a good carpet and fine Venetian glass was much more important than worrying about her own comfort.

She wasn't sure when the business might start making money. The idea of having to meet a payroll every week was frightening, even if it was only for three people. She had supplies to buy and rent to pay and advertising to place in *Vogue* and other similar publications.

Elizabeth Arden, the dreamer, bought the finest ingredients for her products and the finest appointments for her salon. Elizabeth Arden, the practical businesswoman, decided not to hire a cleaning crew. She would do that work herself before any of her employees arrived in the morning.

To get her business launched, she set a backbreaking schedule for herself. She arrived at the salon by 7 a.m. to give it a thorough scrubbing and polishing. By the time her employees arrived at 8:30, the place was sparkling and she had put on a freshly starched white coat, ready for the first facial.

Customer appointments started at 9 a.m. and continued until 6 p.m. Irene Delaney, whom Elizabeth called Lanie, would chase her around with a glass of milk and a sandwich at lunchtime. But Elizabeth seldom took time to eat. After she dismissed the staff at 6:30 she went into the back room. There she made up batches of her products and experimented with new ideas.

Later in the evening, she balanced the books and made notes about items in the salon that needed attention. Then she went home for dinner and, perhaps, a manicure or two.

No matter how tired she was, she always gave herself a facial and put her hair up in curlers before climbing into bed.

A less industrious or less ambitious woman might not have taken on so much responsibility and

Mud baths were advertised as a cure for rheumatism. This helped to popularize similar treatments for the skin.

work for herself. But Elizabeth saw no other way to proceed. She was finally her own boss, doing something she was sure was going to succeed. At last, she knew what it was she could do to make money and to make a mark in the world.

Her excitement over having her own salon that she could run the way she wanted gave her the energy and drive to keep going eighteen hours a day, six days a week.

She probably didn't notice that she had no social life. Certainly, she didn't have time to miss one. She would occasionally make dinner for some of her employees at her apartment so that they could talk a little more shop but that was about the extent of it.

Elizabeth Arden's instincts for making her salon the hospitable and charming place it was from the very beginning were remarkable. Nothing in her education or early jobs had really trained her to pick out antiques or fabrics or decorative art objects. Years later, she would hire the best professional decorators in the business to design the interiors of her new salons or freshen rooms in the older ones.

But there were elements of this first effort that persisted throughout her long and successful career. The pink she chose for her first reception-room walls became a trademark. The public recognized her products, always packaged prettily in her pink, as Elizabeth Arden beauty products.

Another design that she spontaneously came up with in the short period between her breakup with Mrs. Hubbard and the hurried opening of her own salon still stands as a signature of Elizabeth Arden all over the world. Maybe the idea came to her during her many walks up Fifth Avenue to admire all the mansions that lined her favorite street. She had spent many Sundays studying and daydreaming about life in those urban palaces. There was no question that she wanted to belong on that thoroughfare herself. It was, after all, Elizabeth who insisted that

Imagination, Daring . . .
and Work, Work, Work

she and Mrs. Hubbard rent their space on Fifth Avenue.

Whatever the inspiration, one of the first things Elizabeth Arden spent her brother's money for was to have the outside door of her salon painted a deep, rich red. She then ordered a brass plaque to be inscribed with her new name in flowing cursive writing. She had the polished nameplate mounted on the door. She knew immediately that it was right. It said what she wanted it to say about her salon.

The red door with its brass plaque is still a distinctive Elizabeth Arden salon signature.

Elizabeth Hits the Big Time

Mrs. Elizabeth Arden's first salon was opened for business in 1910. Although all she could offer her customers at the time were facial treatments, the salon was almost an immediate success.

There is no question that Elizabeth's hard work was as important as any other ingredient in keeping the business going. In the beginning, she often couldn't make the payroll at the end of a week *and* still pay for her advertisements. That's when she would borrow from the Ogilvie sisters on Friday and pay them back on Tuesday. She refused to give up her ads. If she had been obliged to pay a cleaning woman and a porter as well, she might not have succeeded so soon.

She continued to give manicures at night for two more years. One reason she would not give up the extra income was her pride. She was determined to

Elizabeth Hits the Big Time

At the turn of the century, the ideal of beauty was the elegant but mischievous Gibson Girl, created by artist Charles Dana Gibson.

pay back her brother as soon as possible. She wanted him to respect her as a businesswoman whether he understood her ideas or not.

The other reason was that she could not resist investing in the ambiance of her salon. She continued to add beautiful objects to the decor and maintain its upkeep. She believed this was a key to the salon's success.

Elizabeth paid back her brother within six months, and she attracted more and more customers from the society world that she had been cultivating. Her instincts served her well in this early period when there was such a limit on what she could offer in the way of beauty aids.

Women's beauty was measured against the natural good looks of celebrities like Alice Roosevelt, President Theodore Roosevelt's lively daughter, and theatrical stars who—in spite of their makeup—projected a glowing, spiritual quality that had to appear God-given.

The ideal American woman for the first decade of the twentieth century was the creation of Charles Dana Gibson, an artist who thought of himself as a political and social satirist. Gibson's ink drawings appeared in a humor magazine called *Life*. His American girl, based on his wife, the famous beauty Irene Langhorne, became known as the Gibson girl. Never meant to be a paragon, she was embraced by women and men alike as the perfect modern American woman.

The Gibson girl was tall and stately, she was superbly dressed, and she was intelligent and mischievous without being wicked. Women copied her upswept hairdo with a becoming curl on the forehead and an artful wisp or two escaping at the nape of the neck.

This created a particular challenge for anyone in the fledgling beauty business. Practitioners had to promise the natural loveliness of the Gibson girl with only a few face oils and astringents to help them.

Certainly, Elizabeth could not offer products or massage much different from her competitors. What she was shrewd enough to understand was that she could distinguish her salon by making it more pleasant and enjoyable to visit. If women felt pampered and special at Elizabeth Arden's, they would feel better and look better, no matter what kind of facial they received.

But society was changing. As women entered the work force and began to build independent lives for themselves, it was becoming more acceptable to help nature along. And the fashion in beauty was becoming a bit more robust.

Women also were beginning to organize more militantly for their political rights. They wanted suffrage, the right to vote. More than one parade of suffragettes had marched down Fifth Avenue past the salon since its opening.

At first Elizabeth was simply annoyed. It kept customers away when the streets were full of march-

The issue of women's suffrage grew in importance as women became more independent and demanded equal rights.

ing women. Politics had never been important to her. And, of course, she was still a Canadian citizen.

But then she began to sense that there was more to the suffragette movement than just the vote. It represented a change in how women perceived themselves in society. And, it was becoming fashionable in the very world of women she wanted as clients.

When, in 1912, Elizabeth read that a major Fifth Avenue parade of suffragettes was being led by such leaders of society as Mrs. O.H.P. Belmont and Mrs. Otis Skinner, she decided to join them. Close to 15,000 women gathered only a block from the salon. Their meeting place was in front of the newly-built New York Public Library, which took up two blocks on Fifth Avenue from 40th Street to 42nd Street. The spectators that afternoon were said to number almost half a million.

Among the freedoms women were taking for themselves in this new atmosphere were the right to smoke and to attend public functions without escorts—and the right to improve their appearances. It was in 1912 that *Vogue* suggested that a little rouge, discretely used, might make a woman look healthier and younger.

Elizabeth Arden was not far behind the fashion magazine. She started experimenting with tinted powders and rouges in her workroom. It was during these first experiments with makeup colors that she came to realize that she had a particularly good eye for the subtleties of different shades. This made it possible for her not only to create becoming colors for her products, but also to match them skillfully to each woman's individual skin tones.

She used herself as a guinea pig at first, but soon realized that she could get a more objective view by applying her colors to other people. She pressed her employees into service.

As soon as the last client left at night, Elizabeth put Lanie and her other employees into the treatment chairs and began applying her powders and gels. She did their faces over and over again, trying to refine the process of application. She didn't want the makeup to show. She wanted it to add such a natural blush that no one would suspect that it was anything more than the glow of good health.

It wasn't enough just to perfect her own abilities. She had to be sure that each of the women giving treatments could apply the makeup with equal dexterity. This attention to the training of her staff was basic to the success of her enterprise, Elizabeth felt.

At last she was ready to offer her makeup to her clients. She didn't advertise this new service openly. If she knew a customer was attending a particularly important event, Elizabeth might suggest a makeup application for that night. Frequently, when the client agreed, she was rewarded when friends and acquaintances at the party would ask what she had been doing to make her look so happy and well.

Word-of-mouth sold Elizabeth Arden's makeup applications from the very beginning. And the addition of makeup to her line began to put her out in front of the competition. This proof that her approach was correct was a great relief to Elizabeth. She celebrated by raising her prices.

Elizabeth also realized that the newly independent working women were beginning to see cosmetics as an important adjunct to their freedom to improve themselves. She noticed that the cosmetic counters at the big department stores near her salon were getting more prominent displays and were attracting more and more customers.

She went to talk to the cosmetics buyer at Stern's on 42nd Street. He was dubious, but agreed to try some samples of her Venetian beauty creams and skin tonic.

To his amazement, but not Elizabeth's, he sold out the samples immediately and had customers clamoring for more. Elizabeth was elated with the news and decided to spread her marketing wings a little farther down Fifth Avenue to Bonwit Teller's. Her Venetian products were just as popular there.

Word of Elizabeth Arden beauty products was radiating beyond the New York metropolitan area. Orders were coming in from Boston, Washington, D.C., and Philadelphia. She began to worry about her capacity to produce the quantity she needed in her existing space.

By 1914, Elizabeth had acknowledged her success by adding to her staff at the salon and dropping the Mrs. from her name. Florence Nightingale Graham had become Miss Elizabeth Arden, even to herself. She had given up her private manicuring business, and she had even hired a porter.

❋

Florence Nightingale Graham had become Miss Elizabeth Arden, even to herself.

Her energies now were concentrated on expansion. She simply never doubted that the industry she was pioneering would continue to grow and prosper. She just didn't want to fall behind.

She found the new attitude of women about themselves to be exciting. She liked their growing ability to assert themselves and admired their desire to make the most of themselves. She also saw it as an opportunity for her to sell more products.

It was all happening so fast that it was hard for her to decide which route to go. She could open a second salon. She could manufacture more of her existing Venetian products and increase the number of outlets where they were sold. Or she could take a research trip to Europe to find the secrets of its beauty business and turn these secrets into new products.

Elizabeth decided to do them all. She thought they were all important, and she was accustomed to working hard. She had the energy to explore all three options. What she didn't have was enough cash.

This time Elizabeth Arden didn't go to her brother for a loan. She was a respected businesswoman now with her own credit rating, and she went to a bank.

The bank officer assigned to her account was a dapper man with a trim mustache and a ready smile. His name was Thomas Jenkins Lewis and he made no impression on Elizabeth Arden at all. A bachelor in his late thirties, Tom Lewis paid more than passing attention to the pretty young entrepreneur who wanted a loan to expand her thriving beauty emporium. The first expansion project was to open a second salon. From all the interest that had been shown in her products and treatments in different cities, Elizabeth was most taken with the idea of serving the important hostesses in the nation's capital.

She started modestly in Washington, D.C., by renting a treatment room in the back of an exclusive dress shop. It was small but it had her red door as an entryway. She personally trained the treatment women who would work there, and she sent her beloved Lanie down to oversee the new salon's management in the beginning. Again, her instincts were correct. It was an immediate success.

Lanie did such a good job in Washington, D.C., that Elizabeth decided that she could leave her assistant in charge of the New York salon when it became necessary. This made Elizabeth's first trip to Europe a real possibility. If she didn't have to worry about the salons, then she could concentrate on looking into all the beauty culturists her well-traveled New York clients raved about in Paris and Berlin and Vienna.

Elizabeth Arden paid about as much attention to world news as she did to politics. On June 28, 1914, the heir apparent to the Austrian throne, Archduke Francis Ferdinand, and his wife were assassinated in Sarajevo, Bosnia, by a Serbian radical. It was the act that precipitated World War I in Europe.

Elizabeth, however, was too busy opening her salon in the nation's capital that July to pay attention to such a faraway event. She was devoting her attention to how well Lanie could handle the day-to-day management of a beauty-treatment center.

Elizabeth Hits the Big Time

Satisfied that Lanie was a good surrogate, Elizabeth then made plans to sail to France in early August as the first stop on her research trip. She booked second-class passage on a ship scheduled to land in Cherbourg, France. She saw no point in paying the extra money for first class, as she did not intend to join in the social activities. Her goal was to teach herself French during the voyage.

Alone in her small quarters aboard ship, she found that her ability to learn French was not unlike her skill with Mr. Remington's shift-key typewriter. Elizabeth Arden, a little more mature and responsible than Florence Graham had been when she was defeated by the typewriting machine, kept trying. But she never learned to speak the language fluently.

Alone and uncomfortable with the language, Elizabeth arrived in Paris in mid-August. It was a city still in the pristine glory of its Belle Epoque, that era at the turn of the century when many extravagant buildings were erected. Heavy motor traffic had not yet spoiled the walks along its river, the Seine.

She was able to enjoy the glories of one of the world's most beautiful cities the same way she had enjoyed discovering Fifth Avenue in New York.

However, talk of the impending war made her realize that she had better get on with her business. Picking up the English newspapers, she came to see that she would not travel to Berlin or Vienna, and it was unlikely that she would even be able to get passage to London.

In fact, it was not clear how long it would be safe to stay in Paris. She had a Canadian-British passport, and the British were part of the impending conflict.

Elizabeth made lists of all the Paris beauty salons and then made as many as four appointments a day for treatments. As an American visitor, she could ask for samples of each establishment's products to take home with her. The proprietors didn't mind the idea of their special preparations being talked about in New York.

She was impressed with the variety of beauty treatments and preparations offered in this world capital. She was impressed, too, with the number of successful salons. She collected samples of all the makeup, skin products, and perfumes she could find. By the end of a day's work, she was ready for a light supper and bed—but only after she made careful notes about each place and each product.

It is more than likely that Elizabeth visited a new salon in Paris that became all the rage that year. Named Maison de Beauté Valaze, it was run by a woman who called herself Helena Rubinstein. Her most popular products were a line of herbal preparations for the skin. Elizabeth Arden surely bought samples.

Toward the end of her stay in Paris, Elizabeth wanted to have dinner in one of the more elegant restaurants to see how fashionable Parisians dressed at night. She chose the Café de Paris on the Rue de la Paix.

It was not far from her hotel, and she thought it would be pleasant to walk there. It was a warm September evening. She strolled through the Place Vendôme with its stately old buildings and large open square, one of the most elegant streets in the world. Without an escort and without a real command of French, she probably did not feel at home, but she must have responded to its grandeur. She could not have guessed that her own name would one day be found there.

At dinner she discovered two interesting things. One was that the smart set in Paris was dancing the fox-trot and the Castle Walk, two steps introduced to them by the popular American dancers Irene and Vernon Castle. The second and more important thing she noticed was that the women were wearing mascara and eye shadow.

What impressed Elizabeth was that the eye makeup was so carefully applied that at first she did not recognize it. She just saw pretty eyes. In New

York, not even actresses wore eye makeup off the stage. It was too dark and dramatic to look natural, except under very bright lights.

Elizabeth had not seen eye makeup in any of the salons she had visited. She spent the next day going to shops looking for samples of mascara and eye shadow. What she found didn't satisfy her. It was like theatrical makeup.

She turned her hotel room into a laboratory and started experimenting. She used one of the hotel maids as a reluctant model. Although she did not come up with the perfect combination there in the hotel, she came close enough to feel confident that she could perfect a delicate but effective eye makeup for her clients.

Elizabeth was very pleased at the thought of introducing eye makeup to American society women. She was so pleased, in fact, that she forgot about the maid, who was anxious to be allowed to go home. In her frustration, the poor maid had started to cry. Black streaks rolled down her cheeks as the mascara mixed with her tears.

Elizabeth was faced with the fact about the first mascara formulas. They ran. She never did manage to make mascara waterproof by herself. It would be many years before a competitor would manage that, and Elizabeth would have to copy the rival's product.

The war news got worse. Elizabeth had to scramble to get a berth on a ship bound for New York. Finally, she got a place on an English liner, *Lusitania*, sailing at the end of September.

She was ready to go home. She had suitcases full of new product ideas. She was anxious to start work on her eye makeup in her own laboratory. And she was tired of trying to communicate in French.

She probably wouldn't have admitted it even to herself, but she also must have been very lonely.

Time Out for Romance

*T*he ship was filled to
capacity for the trip back to New York. The war was
spreading rapidly and American citizens, since their
country was not yet involved, wanted to return to the
safety of their own shores.

Danger on the high seas was a reality for an
English liner. German submarines, called U-boats,
were already threatening shipping in European
waters. These underwater vessels had torpedoed
and destroyed a number of ships in the North Atlantic Ocean.

Black curtains covered all the portholes at night
to keep the *Lusitania* from being sighted by enemy
ships. Inside, the passengers—unable to do anything to defend themselves—took a "devil-may-
care" attitude and put their energies into enjoying
themselves.

The first night out, Elizabeth was sitting alone at
a table for two in the dining room. A trim, well-

dressed man asked if he might join her. The room was too crowded for her to say no. Besides, he seemed pleasant enough. He was an American in his late thirties, and he seemed terribly friendly.

His conversation was witty and fun and she enjoyed it. But she was bewildered by his familiarity with her. Why would a stranger know so much about her, she wondered. The man continued to tease her through dinner. When he finally realized that she did not recognize him at all, he told her who he was.

"Miss Arden," he said, "I'm the man who okayed your loan at the bank." This time Elizabeth paid attention to Tom Lewis. He was charming and a fun companion. He danced with her after dinner and invited her for lunch the next day.

Soon they were spending all their time together on the ship. Elizabeth was having a wonderful time, and they became a popular couple for other people to invite to shipboard parties. The woman whose business it was to make other women as attractive and appealing as they could be was having her own turn as belle of the ball.

Tom Lewis was clearly attracted to her and wanted to continue to see her when they returned to New York. Elizabeth wasn't so sure she could mix work with this kind of pleasure. She had big plans for her business, and she wasn't sure she would have time for seeing a man, too.

Elizabeth liked Tom Lewis. But she still had strong feelings against love and marriage because of her mother. She was achieving just the independence and economic stability she had always wanted. She wouldn't risk that for anyone, so she refused to see him.

She didn't miss him so much at first. She wanted to have all her Paris samples analyzed. She turned first to Parke-Davis, the chemical company that supplied her with the ingredients for her home-made Venetian products. But they refused to look at the Paris samples.

✳

The woman whose business it was to make other women attractive was having her own turn as belle of the ball.

Parke-Davis already had what they considered to be more serious medical and industrial contracts to fulfill, and they really didn't believe that cosmetics were important enough to justify time and attention. They suggested she try a smaller firm.

At Stillwell and Gladding, chemical analysts, Elizabeth met with one of the partners, A. Fabian Swanson. He listened with rapt attention to her story of her company, her trip to Paris, and her plans for expansion. He was enchanted with Elizabeth and her enthusiasm. The two seemed to have an instant rapport.

He presented her proposal to the other partners. They, like Parke-Davis, felt cosmetics were a frivolous business for scientists and didn't want to become involved. However, they respected Swanson and didn't want to lose him, so they compromised. His partners allowed him to make a private contract with Elizabeth and to use their laboratory after hours to work on the analyses of her creams and tonics and perfumes.

Soon they both knew the secrets of all the French beauty products Elizabeth had brought back from Paris. Elizabeth had grown to trust and admire Swanson. She decided that, with his help, they could do something better than just copy her overseas competition. To her, although many of the French creams were superior to the current American products, none were really ideal. She saw the problem as consistency. The creams were all hard and oily.

Having a sympathetic scientist to work with was very exciting to Elizabeth. She knew her limitations in the laboratory. But now she could tell him what she thought a good product should be. He had the knowledge to try and create it.

"I want a face cream that is light and fluffy, almost like whipped cream," she told Swanson.

He took up the challenge and returned to his laboratory. It took several months, but one afternoon he appeared at the salon with a sample jar of what looked like beaten egg whites. In addition to its delicate consistency, the cream had a fresh and delightful odor.

Elizabeth tried it herself first. It melted into her skin and left no oily residue. Next she tried it on her employees with the same happy results. Everyone in the salon knew they had a winning new product. It was pleasant to apply, it left skin feeling soft, and it gave off a light, clean smell.

She named it Venetian Cream Amoretta. And to make sure no one would think it came out of a mundane New York chemical laboratory, she advertised it as "a famous French formula containing the perfume of delicate May flowers." Beauty products, she felt then, had more appeal if they had mysterious and exotic origins. Simple chemistry was not enough.

Venetian Cream Amoretta was an immediate success. Elizabeth commissioned Swanson to come up with a companion face lotion much gentler than her own or her competition's. When he succeeded with that project, Elizabeth felt she had made a real breakthrough in skin care.

To celebrate, she devised a name that would make it impossible for clients to confuse her product with anyone else's. Mrs. Adair's Ganesh products might be confused with Mrs. Hubbard's Grecian products. But Elizabeth's new lotion was called Ardena Skin Tonic. She was to use Ardena in creating many future labels.

The success of the two new products created new problems. Swanson, whose laboratory was downtown, brought batches of the facial preparations up to the salon on the Third Avenue elevated train. At first it was easy because the quantities were small enough to fit into gallon jugs that he could carry under his arms. But as the orders got larger and his carrying vessels more ungainly, he began to dread the trips on the "el," as the trains were called. The vats became heavier and heavier. Sometimes the guards tried to keep him and his vats off the train because they took up too much room.

Swanson finally appealed to Elizabeth. She hired a messenger to transport his fresh batches. Demand kept growing, however, so she ended up with a truck.

Her clientele at the salon was growing, too. So Elizabeth took larger quarters on the fourth floor of 509 Fifth Avenue. She called the new space Salon d'Oro, the room of gold. Part of her former space was turned into stockrooms, from which she filled product orders.

She tried a new enterprise in the rest of the old salon space. Elizabeth had always believed that the more versatile her business was in meeting women's needs, the more distinctive and successful the salon would be. She had certainly been right about the benefits to all when she joined forces with the Ogilvie sisters. Being connected with a milliner had been an advantage. So now she wanted to have her own dressmaking enterprise.

She relied on her own tastes as a designer and hired seamstresses to execute and fit her creations. This time Elizabeth had spread her talents too far. Her designs were not a success, and she closed this part of the operation before its first anniversary. She, at least, could recognize a failure and cut her losses—for the moment anyway. Much later she would enter the world of high fashion.

She fared better with her introduction of eye makeup. It was for the daring few, but they were indeed Arden customers and they were the fashion-setters of New York. Eye makeup soon became the trend-setting way for partygoers to do their faces.

Except for the dressmaking, Elizabeth was scoring one success after another. The Washington, D.C., salon was prospering, the enlarged Salon d'Oro in New York was booked days in advance, and she was receiving orders for her products from all over the eastern seaboard.

She rewarded herself by moving into a larger apartment on Riverside Drive.

If she missed Tom Lewis, she had very little time to think about it. Absorbed in her eighteen-hour days of new and exciting challenges at the salon, she showed no signs of regret at having stopped seeing him. Her colleagues probably didn't even know about her shipboard romance.

The last months of 1914 and the early months of 1915 were one of Elizabeth's happiest times of expansion in the business. Perhaps she believed her own advertising copy, which she often wrote herself. She touted the New York salon as being "where the spirit of youth is so all pervading that you cannot leave without catching some of it."

On May 8, 1915, the *Lusitania*, the ship that Elizabeth and Tom had met on, was sunk off the coast of Ireland by a German U-boat. A thousand people died, including 114 Americans. It seriously imperiled the United States' neutrality in the war, although it would be another two years before Americans officially entered World War I.

The luxury liner Lusitania, *torpedoed by a German U-boat, sank in eighteen minutes.*

As soon as he heard about the *Lusitania*, Tom called up Elizabeth. He told her about the tragedy. It could have been them, he reminded her. Shouldn't they see it as an omen of their good fortune that they weren't drowned? He definitely thought they should at least celebrate their own survival.

Elizabeth relented and said yes. She began seeing Tom several nights a week. When he showed up at the salon one afternoon in uniform, ready to join the fighting forces in Europe, she realized she didn't want to lose him again.

She agreed to marry Tom Lewis—but on her own schedule. The day of the wedding, she treated herself to a facial and makeup application, let the Ogilvies fix her hair, and took a whole hour off in the afternoon to have the ceremony performed. Then she returned to the salon to finish out the working day. She met her new husband for dinner, and they spent their wedding night at the St. Regis Hotel.

Tom went off to war, and Elizabeth returned to running her business. Swanson continued to produce new products to her specifications. Venetian Cream Amoretta was followed by Venetian Pore Cream for treating blackheads. Next, Venetian Lille Lotion claimed to help a fair-skinned woman keep from freckling. Then, Venetian Muscle Oil was supposed to be an antidote to wrinkles; while Venetian Adona Cream was designed to firm up sagging necks and busts. Venetian Velva Cream was a new emollient for dry skin. Elizabeth's line of rouges and tinted face powders offered more and more colors.

Mrs. Hubbard had gone out of business. Mrs. Adair, in an effort to compete with Elizabeth Arden, had given an Eastern flavor to her advertisements. She now claimed that her Ganesh products were named for a Hindu god of wisdom. She learned the secret of her muscle cream near his temple in India, she wrote. It did not convince the social set, who were making a ritual of their appointments at Elizabeth Arden's salon.

Time Out for Romance

Elizabeth—a good ten years older than anyone around her suspected—sold youth more than mystery. A *Vogue* ad she wrote in 1915 had a drawing of a pretty matron with teacup in hand. "My dear!" she is saying, "She looks so much older!" The ad goes on to point out how unnecessary wrinkles and sagging can add years to a woman's age. Elizabeth concludes her pitch by writing "... there is really not an iota of an excuse for a woman of today to lose one bit of her youthful attractiveness. For every woman can do what hundreds of Miss Arden's clients have done for years, and keep the skin and complexion in the pink of condition, the facial contour firm, well-molded, and youthful by devoting ten minutes each day to proper treatment with the Venetian products."

Elizabeth Arden seemed to be the unchallenged leader of the new beauty industry. Companies like Palmolive and Ponds did a greater volume of business to a much wider market, but their products were not yet considered to be real beauty preparations. They were simple utilitarian creams carried by pharmacies and variety stores across the country. These large companies were not in the business of selling dreams.

An occasional competitor appeared on the New York scene and disappeared. The music-hall star Lillian Russell, for example, tried to use her fabled beauty to promote a line of cosmetics. Times had changed since she was the toast of Broadway, and it was a short-lived enterprise.

For a brief period Elizabeth Arden did reign supreme in the business she helped to invent. But most successful people are not allowed to go unchallenged for very long.

For all the money that she had made in her first five remarkable years, Elizabeth Arden was not the first self-made millionairess in the United States. That honor was won by a woman eleven years Elizabeth's senior who made her fortune in another part of the same business.

She called herself Madame C.J. Walker, and she was born in 1867 to two former black slaves. She started her cosmetics business on "$2 and a dream." Her first product was a hair pomade for black women which she claimed would drive away the "nappy-headed blues."

Madame Walker started her business in Indianapolis, Indiana, the same year Elizabeth Arden opened her salon in New York. Madame Walker sold her products out of a suitcase in the beginning, giving careful demonstrations of how each should be used and lecturing on its benefits.

As her line of products and her reputation grew, she began to train young black women to go out as her salesforce. She taught her representatives how to give hair treatments and facials to their customers and how to sell.

Madame C. J. Walker (left), being given a manicure by one of her trained staff. Several of her products can be seen in the foreground.

Her success was astonishing, and this self-taught, uneducated black businesswoman immediately poured her proceeds back into her community by providing training and jobs for more and more young black women.

In the first decades of this century, the only jobs black women could get were in other people's homes at less pay than white domestic servants could command. Madame Walker created sales jobs, factory jobs, bookkeeping jobs, and secretarial jobs at decent wages for a whole army of black people. Graduates of her beauty "colleges," as she called her schools, took Walker's twenty-three creams and tonics all over the northeastern United States.

She was a woman of energy and imagination, much like Elizabeth Arden, but her mission was to make a whole generation of black people self-confident and financially independent.

In 1917 Madame Walker hired a black architect to build her a villa on the Hudson River in Irvington, New York. She did not live to enjoy it long, but her daughter A'Lelia gave Sunday concerts there to showcase black musicians for a mixed audience of New York cultural leaders.

Madame Walker died in 1919 with many of her plans unrealized. The Walker Building in Indianapolis was completed by her business heirs as a factory for her products and a theater and social center for her people.

Her company did not survive the 1930s economic depression in the United States.

While Elizabeth Arden never had reason to see Madame Walker as a competitor, she did recognize as a rival another cosmetics entrepreneur who called herself Madame. Just as Elizabeth was congratulating herself on her undisputed leadership in the new industry, Helena Rubinstein emigrated to the United States.

Chapter *8*

"That Woman"

When Elizabeth Arden took her first trip to Paris at the beginning of World War I, she had visited every beauty salon in the city that she could find. Among them must have been Helena Rubinstein's Maison de Beauté Valaze.

It was one of the most popular and successful salons in Paris and was, in fact, Madame Rubinstein's second House of Beauty. The original was still flourishing in London.

The owner of these establishments was a woman close to Elizabeth's age whose career was not too different. She, too, had seen the potential for a business built on the promise of preserving women's youthful good looks. Madame Rubinstein had carefully nurtured her concept into a lucrative line of products and treatments. She simply had done it in another part of the world.

The woman who called herself Madame Helena Rubinstein was born in Krakow, Poland, around 1882. (Not unlike Elizabeth, she guarded her age as carefully as she guarded the formulas for her cosmetics.) Her family was middle class and Jewish, and she was encouraged to get an education.

Her father, a merchant, wanted her to go to medical school. She enjoyed the laboratory work, but hated being around sick people and serious illnesses. She quit medical school and, to escape her father's wrath, went to live in Australia with a sympathetic uncle.

Madame Rubinstein, like Elizabeth, had been blessed with a creamy and flawless complexion. She was dismayed by the sun-scorched, roughened skin of the women in Australia. She had brought with her a supply of a skin cream that a doctor in her home town supplied to a small circle of customers.

She opened a small shop and began to sell the idea of skin care as a basis for youth and beauty along with small jars of the doctor's concoction. Demand for the cream was so great that she eventually persuaded him to give up his practice in Krakow and join her in Australia.

With the doctor as her consultant, Madame Rubinstein advertised herself as a skin-care specialist. The response was such that she made more than $100,000 the first year. That was an extraordinary amount of money in the first decade of this century when the average wage was 22 cents an hour.

After amassing a sizable fortune in Australia, Madame Rubinstein decided it was time to try her luck in a more sophisticated and exciting part of the world. She moved to London and rented a house in the fashionable Mayfair district. The house belonged to the British prime minister, Lord Salisbury.

She, like her counterparts in New York, played on the romance of foreign names and called her first European salon Maison de Beauté Valaze. She appealed to wealthy, upper-class women. The decor of her salon was sumptuous and bold. She relied more on paintings and other works of art than on the antiques that Elizabeth Arden preferred, but the effect of luxury was similar.

Although she herself stayed faithful to her original Krakow face cream, she offered her customers a variety of products and treatments. She was the first to popularize herbal products in skin care.

In London she met and married an American newspaperman, Edward J. Titus. The couple had two sons before she expanded her empire to Paris, where she opened the salon that Elizabeth Arden probably visited in 1914.

With the outbreak of World War I in Europe, she decided to move her family to the safety of the United States. (Like Elizabeth, she gained American citizenship with her marriage to an American.)

Embarking in New York, she is reputed to have remarked immediately on the paleness of American women's faces, the grayness of their lips, and the prominence of their noses, purple with cold. Her reaction seems to have been that her new country offered a huge market for her products.

She set about looking for a proper location for a salon. Within a few months she had picked a building at 15 East 49th Street, just off Fifth Avenue, seven blocks north of Elizabeth Arden's Salon d'Oro. She took a full-page ad in *Vogue* to announce the opening of her New York Maison de Beauté Valaze.

Elizabeth Arden saw this as a direct challenge to her business. She looked for new and larger quarters herself and managed to find a space with a private entrance at Fifth Avenue and 53rd Street.

Girding herself for a long-term war, not just a brief battle, Elizabeth also took new rooms for her wholesale business and her own laboratory. She persuaded Swanson to quit Stillwell and Gladding and join her full time.

The verbal contest between the cosmetic tycoons took place on the pages of the fashion maga-

Helena Rubinstein (1871– 1965) opened her first beauty salon in London in 1908. She was Elizabeth Arden's greatest rival.

zines. In the early days of their rivalry, there were no laws governing truth in advertising. Madame Rubinstein described herself as "the greatest living beauty exponent in the world." Elizabeth claimed she had "given her life to the study of this subject both here and abroad, in Paris, London, and Berlin."

When Helena Rubinstein suggested that her massages restored youthful skin, Elizabeth suggested that massage was a superficial technique and that only her superior products could keep the skin pliant and glowing.

With Swanson's help, Elizabeth quickly took the lead in the number of beauty products she offered. Madame Rubinstein concentrated on opening salons. By 1918 she had Houses of Beauty in Chicago, San Francisco, Philadelphia, New Orleans, and on the boardwalk in the fashionable resort, Atlantic City.

Elizabeth, not to be outdone, established salons in Palm Beach, Florida; Newport, Rhode Island; Boston, and San Francisco.

Other entrepreneurs were entering the beauty field at the same time. One of them, a former Arden employee named Dorothy Grey, blatantly advertised herself as a former partner of Elizabeth's and claimed her products were the originals. Elizabeth retaliated with ads setting the record straight, but Dorothy Grey was an irritant, not a real threat.

Helena Rubinstein was as strong, shrewd, and single-minded as Elizabeth, and Elizabeth knew it. They would goad each other for forty years, even after other competitors threatened to dominate the field they had pioneered.

Beyond their own ambitions—which were enormous—they probably did more to spur each other's expansion than any other single factor.

Their rivalry started in New York, but it became worldwide before they were through. Their lives had many parallels; and they probably would have been more capable of understanding each other than anyone else who knew either of them.

By their own design, they never met.

In fact, they never even uttered each other's names. They referred to each other as "that woman." Their feud became legendary in their industry. Some twenty years later, an upstart cosmetics entrepreneur, Charles Revson, mocked them both by naming one of his popular perfumes "That Woman." That may have annoyed them, but his real transgression was outselling them both with his Revlon products.

The arrival of Helena Rubinstein in New York just as Elizabeth's new husband joined the army kept Elizabeth from really pining for him. She was too busy keeping up with her new competitor. She also was fighting her old hip injury, which had flared up painfully again.

Dissatisfied with the ministrations of her doctors, which gave her no relief, she found some practitioners of yoga in her neighborhood. Impressed with their ability to transcend physical pain, she began studying with them. She did find relief and she found the basis for a whole new area of activity in her salons, exercise.

The war came to an end in late 1918 with the signing of the Armistice on November 11. Tom Lewis came home to a wife he hardly knew, who had become an even more dedicated career woman. Elizabeth was very conscious of her success and had no inclination to share it with him—or with her family, for that matter. Her sister Gladys had come to New York to recover from a bad marriage and hoped to work for Elizabeth.

Elizabeth seemed reluctant to involve either of them in the business at first. But the pressure of opening new salons to keep up with Madame Rubinstein was making her neglect the wholesale part of the business, which Tom and Gladys felt could be expanded quite profitably.

A run-in with an auditor who did not like the way she kept her books made Elizabeth turn to Tom Lewis, the former banker. Little by little he made

Elizabeth Arden and her pet German Shepherd "Don Caesar" in Southampton, Long Island, in 1922.

himself more and more indispensible in the parts of the enterprise that she least enjoyed.

He and Gladys felt they could sell Elizabeth Arden products in many more places if they tried. Gladys wanted to take the creams, lotions, and makeup on the road and demonstrate them across the country where they were not well known. Needing more cash to put into the new salons, Elizabeth finally agreed to let them try it.

Gladys proved herself to be almost as good a saleswoman as her sister. Everywhere she went she caused excitement and rang up sales. She began training saleswomen in the stores where she introduced the Arden products so that they could demonstrate how to use the various creams and lotions properly. Customers loved the demonstrations, and the stores loved the increased traffic.

Soon Gladys was training teams of traveling cosmetics demonstrators and saleswomen. Elizabeth appreciated the care with which Gladys chose and taught the Arden representatives. They were attractive, well-spoken, and charming young women and they created a demand for the products beyond Elizabeth's expectations.

She began to see her sister as an asset to the business rather than a threat. That gave her another idea. Now that the war was over, she wanted to match her new rival in Madame Rubinstein's own territory—Europe.

Under the guise of a belated honeymoon, she and Tom planned a trip to London. At the same time she agreed to send Gladys to Paris as a treat. Her sister had always been a Francophile and spoke the language—with the Canadian cadences, of course—fluently.

In truth, Elizabeth wanted to try to sell Arden products in both countries, if possible. She and Tom would take England, and Gladys, who had indeed been promised a vacation, would see what the possibilities in France might be.

Elizabeth and Tom found the English to be snobbish about American products. They looked down their noses at them. They had their own Yardley and Floris products, Madame Rubinstein's line, and some French imports, and they weren't really interested in anything from the United States.

They found a sympathetic buyer at the great British department store Harrod's, a man named Edward Haslam, who suggested they try selling first in the provincial cities. There the landed gentry shopped. If the gentry took an interest in Arden products in the country, they would then request them in London. That would build the market.

It sounded like a long and difficult route to Tom, but Elizabeth liked Haslam and trusted him. It did take time, but eventually the plan worked and Haslam became head of Elizabeth Arden in England not too many years later.

Gladys had a more heartening experience in Paris. She figured out immediately that the two great department stores were the most fashionable places to introduce a new line of cosmetics. She could try Galeries Lafayette or Au Printemps. By chance, she was first able to get an appointment with Raul Mayer, the head of Galeries Lafayette.

The short, slim styles of the 1920s inspired women to exercise. Diet programs, such as the one promoted by Arden, also kept women trim.

Mayer was charmed by the little Canadian and agreed to let her open a stall—at her expense—in his store to try to sell her products. The experiment went well. After a few weeks, Gladys was able to train an assistant to take over the counter while she went to the fashionable resort area in the south of France, the Riviera, to find outlets there.

Gladys was doing so well that she extended her stay. She loved France, and she was comfortable there. She was selling Arden products so successfully that she began to look for warehouse space. Her weeks rolled into months and soon it became clear that she really didn't want to return to New York.

Elizabeth could not have had a better French representative. Within a year Gladys had opened a salon in Paris; and shortly after another followed in Nice on the Riviera. It was Gladys who realized how much the company would save by having its own manufacturing plant in France. She supervised its opening, and Tom then established similar plants in other countries when demand became high enough.

The 1920s were a boom time for the cosmetics business on both sides of the Atlantic. People really

Hats, gloves, and silk stockings were essential to the fashionable looks of the 1920s. The fox stole was also popular.

believed that World War I, the "war to end wars," had done just that. There was optimism and a sense of freedom and relief.

Women had gained the vote in the United States and in many other countries and, during the war, they had gained a sense of independence and self-reliance. They wanted to work hard and play hard, and most of all they wanted to look good doing both.

Taboos on makeup no longer existed. Everybody wanted to look young and energetic. The Elizabeth Ardens and Helena Rubinsteins were only limited by their own imaginations on what they might create and sell to these liberated women.

Elizabeth opened her London salon at 25 Old Bond Street, and Tom opened a British factory.

The Arden product line continued to expand. Freed from her agreement with the Ogilvie sisters, Elizabeth launched a whole new series of shampoos and hair tonics along with a new set of bath products.

She became more imaginative in her selling and advertising, too. She was the first to offer a whole variety of lipstick colors to match a woman's outfits and not just her skin.

Gladys found her a French perfume line that allowed Elizabeth Arden to sell scents for different occasions—one for daytime or business wear, another for afternoon social events, and still a third for evening wear.

It was in the 1920s that Elizabeth first recorded a beauty phonograph record. It gave instructions for doing yoga exercises. It was a great success, and it was not long afterward that she opened the first exercise room in one of her salons.

The Elizabeth Arden Company was grossing more than 2 million dollars a year just in the United States in the 1920s. Elizabeth and Tom—each taking care of a different part of her business—were the toast of New York. People wanted them at their receptions and charity parties.

They were charming and successful and enjoying all the attention they attracted. They themselves loved to entertain in their Fifth Avenue apartment, which Elizabeth could now afford. They were popular hosts. The couple seemed to have everything.

But they didn't. Elizabeth still could not trust people in loving relationships. She was suspicious of her husband's role in her business, and she was suspicious of his relationships with other women.

What Tom wanted was trust, respect for his work, and some understanding of his feelings. Those were things Elizabeth couldn't give him.

Bad Times and Big Profits

*B*y the end of the 1920s, Elizabeth Arden may not have been the richest woman in the world—there were heiresses whose fortunes certainly exceeded hers—but she was in a charmed and tiny circle of women who had amassed their own considerable wealth. In 1929 she was offered 15 million dollars for her company.

There were many who thought she ought to take the offer. She could live extravagantly on the proceeds for the rest of her life. And she was, as only she knew, entering her fifties.

Elizabeth wasn't even tempted. Her business was her life. She got no real satisfaction from her marriage. She had no children. And she had no hobbies or consuming interests other than those that pertained to her work.

Her disposition had not mellowed. She was more autocratic than ever. Although she always paid good wages to the people who worked for her, she was a demanding and difficult employer.

Her temper was becoming a real problem, and Tom Lewis was one of the few people who could calm her down. Although she could never apologize in person for being rude or unreasonable to a staff member, she could sometimes be persuaded to send notes and gifts to the person she had mistreated to make amends.

She was enjoying the social part of her life. She had been befriended by Elizabeth Marbury—a woman of impeccable social standing, with a long and distinguished New England pedigree, who seemed the opposite of Elizabeth in every way. Elizabeth Marbury had inherited her money. She was grossly overweight and uninterested in her personal appearance. She was an intellectual who had acted as the agent in America for such writers as George Bernard Shaw, Oscar Wilde, and W. Somerset Maugham when their works were considered to be very controversial. She was active in liberal politics.

Elizabeth Arden was thrilled by the world of the arts and high society that Elizabeth Marbury opened to her. It was Elizabeth Marbury, called Bessie by her friends, who introduced Elizabeth Arden to the famous British photographer and designer Cecil Beaton. It was Bessie who also got Elizabeth interested in collecting art.

Before long, Elizabeth Arden was buying Georgia O'Keeffe paintings and sitting for her own portrait by Augustus John. She wore a designer dress by one of Bessie's friends, Charles James. Elizabeth, being Elizabeth, wasn't pleased by the portrait or the gown and had both changed, to everyone's chagrin. But she would eventually hire James to revive her own dress-design department.

Bessie got Elizabeth interested in charity work, so Elizabeth could sit on boards with the members of high society who continued to be in awe of her. And Bessie introduced Elizabeth and Tom to the quiet beauties of the Belgrade Lakes region of Maine where the Marbury summer house was located.

Soon Bessie encouraged Elizabeth to buy her own estate in Maine. It was a lovely lakefront property of 750 acres with a house that needed rebuilding. Elizabeth took charge of the renovations. Tom named the place Maine Chance.

Elizabeth and Tom were a good business team. She worked on new products and services. He worried about new markets and how to supply them. Soon, her cosmetics were being merchandized in South America, Africa, Asia, and Australia, as well as North America and Europe.

Elizabeth loved to point out to people that there were only three American names known in every corner of the globe: Singer Sewing Machines, Coca-Cola®, and Elizabeth Arden.

Wherever Elizabeth saw that her treatment products (as opposed to makeup)—were doing particularly well, she began investigating the possibility of opening a salon.

It was Tom Lewis who saw that the optimism and excesses of the 1920s in the United States and Western Europe were getting out of hand. People were sure they could make money in anything, and they were borrowing much too much cash without collateral to back it up.

He was concerned about Elizabeth's spending for new salons and factories when the economy looked so unstable. He felt they should not borrow too much money when there was the possibility of a depression.

Elizabeth respected his business sense and thought he might be right about the general economy. But her intuition also told her that the beauty business might well be one of the few industries that could ride out bad times.

She was able to put her theory to the test. The stock market crash hit the United States in October 1929. It was a dramatic symbol of the economic prob-

The Bank of the United States in New York was one of the many banks that closed in 1929, ushering in the Great Depression.

lems that Tom had foreseen. The crash precipitated a panic that threw America and most of the world into the worst economic depression in modern times.

Industrial output plummeted, unemployment rose to alarming numbers, and wages fell. Farmers in the Midwest were hit by low prices and drought. Banks failed. The Metropolitan Life Insurance Company reported that in 1931 more than 20,000 Americans committed suicide. Hunger and poverty were rampant throughout the country.

Elizabeth had been right, however. In 1928, the volume of sales in the U.S. cosmetics industry was 500 million dollars. At the end of 1929 it has risen to 750 million dollars. Her customers—the elite—

could give up summer houses and chauffeurs and elaborate entertaining, but they held on to the small luxuries of a facial or an exercise class or a bottle of expensive hand cream.

The Depression did not slow down the growth of Elizabeth Arden, the business, nor did it dampen the lifestyle of Elizabeth Arden, the woman.

Berlin and Rome were among the sites of new salons. Elizabeth attended the openings and stayed on to look over the European beauty business. She was, as ever, on the lookout for new techniques and new products.

A profile of Elizabeth Arden in *The New Yorker* in 1935 described a day at her New York salon. Between

9 in the morning and 6 at night, 394 women went through the red door now at 691 Fifth Avenue. Most—294 of them—wanted facial treatments of one kind or another.

These ranged from a simple massage to applications of Sensation salve—a kind of mudpack—or a gland cream, to the most costly and elaborate treatment of all: the Vienna Youth Mask. This last treatment Elizabeth had worked out on one of her trips with a Dr. Last in Austria.

It was based on the therapeutic properties of applying heat to human tissue with electric currents, a process called diathermy. Doctors used it to treat arthritis and other inflammatory conditions, but Elizabeth thought it might regenerate skin cells on the face.

Clients sat in a treatment booth at a mirrored dressing table, which was decorated with a vase of fresh flowers. In treatment gowns to protect their clothes, the women had their faces covered with papier-mâché masks lined with tinfoil and connected by wires to an electrical machine. When all was properly in place, the electricity was turned on and the heat applied.

Elizabeth believed that the skin under the eyes and under the chin would benefit most by the Vienna Youth Mask. Doctors were skeptical, but agreed that it was probably good for circulation. Whatever the reason, clients emerged with glowing faces. At the height of the Depression, the Vienna Youth Mask was very popular, and a series of thirty-two treatments cost $200.

Clients who were not in the salon for facials were intent on improving their figures. Elizabeth offered exercise classes based on her yoga experiences. Clients stretched out on satin mats and followed instructions. They were encouraged to do headstands to improve their circulation and posture. Elizabeth herself did daily headstands, believing they were as important to her beauty ritual as her facials. Along with the yoga exercises, there were classes in rhythmic dance and tap.

Other body treatments included massage on a machine with giant rollers and a paraffin bath to induce sweating, which Elizabeth had discovered at a spa in Bavaria. The sweating was reputed to cleanse the pores of poisons and give a glow to the skin, while it also created a temporary weight loss. She employed a staff doctor to screen clients before they were allowed in the bath. The paraffin treatment would have been harmful for people with heart conditions.

Elizabeth also offered her clients a diet designed by a nutritionist that substituted brown sugar for white sugar and emphasized the importance of steamed vegetables.

On the social front, Elizabeth began a series of elaborate house parties at Maine Chance on weekends. Guests would be put up at her house and its guest cottages and then entertained at her friend Bessie's estate.

Bessie Marbury died suddenly in the early 1930s, and Elizabeth grieved. Bessie was probably the closest friend she ever had. (Elizabeth had even, at Bessie's suggestion, given a party in Maine to raise money for the campaign of Franklin D. Roosevelt for president. He, a Democrat, had won and had begun to put regulations on businesses like Elizabeth's, much to her outrage.)

Without Bessie, the Maine property had less personal appeal for Elizabeth. So, at the height of the Depression, she used it to launch one of her most inspired ideas. With the help of a diet adviser, Gaylord Hauser, she turned Maine Chance into a rigorous health spa for wealthy women.

It was a novel idea. Within the beautiful setting of the lakeside mansion and its cottages, she imposed a strict regimen of diet and exercise and beauty treatments for which she charged her guests $100 a day. She added a swimming pool, steam

✳

Elizabeth did daily headstands, believing they were as important to her beauty ritual as her facials.

Bad Times and Big Profits

rooms, and treatment rooms to the estate for the guests' workouts and lavish decor and gardens for their pleasure between beauty regimens.

There was no wine or liquor served, the menus were sparse, and guests were thrown out if they brought any food or alcohol of their own. Concessions were made for no one. Why would people pay so much money to be treated so harshly? The concept was preposterous, but it worked. Exhausted but happy guests, who had worked off five pounds in a week, told their friends about it and the waiting list grew.

Breakfast was served in bed on fine china at the beginning of each day. The English comedienne Bea Lillie described her stay at Maine Chance: "You wake up in the morning with someone pushing a rose in your face. And with it comes the day's schedule: rise at 7:30, breakfast at 8, mud-packs at 8:15, steam baths at 8:30, exercise at 9, hup, two, three, four."

Elizabeth had scored another innovative success that would be copied by many.

As much as she missed her friend Bessie, through her Elizabeth had established a social life that helped the business, satisfied her need for status, and did not demand a husband. She decided to divorce Tom.

Elizabeth never understood or sympathized with Tom's need for appreciation. He was running a part of the business that grossed close to 3 million dollars a year, but she gave him no credit. She fired him from her life and the business with a settlement of only $25,000. For that, he had to agree not to work in the cosmetics business for five years, which he honored. At the same time, she fired her brother William, who had joined the company through Tom's invitation, not hers.

Arrogant and alone, Elizabeth opened Maine Chance with a huge party honoring Bessie Marbury's memory. She brought thirty-five guests up from New York in a private railroad car with a special chef, a hostess to introduce them to each other, musicians, and a heavily stocked bar. She was beginning to throw her money and her power around.

She probably didn't notice the difference in her behavior without Tom's carefully phrased questions and suggestions, which often made her think twice before doing something rash or rude.

Others did notice. Her sister Gladys, who had married Vicomte Henri de Maublanc and settled in France, stopped allowing Elizabeth to stay with her in Paris. Gladys once returned from a trip to discover that Elizabeth had redecorated her sister's whole apartment to suit Elizabeth's taste. Gladys was livid, but Elizabeth couldn't understand why she wasn't grateful.

And her employees felt the difference. Elizabeth did not listen to advice anymore. She decided, for example, that she wanted to sponsor a radio show on NBC featuring Eddy Duchin and his orchestra, the dramatization of a new wedding each week, and a gossip section provided by a society columnist.

Tom Lewis had always advised against advertising Arden products on radio. Their appeal was their exclusivity—the products could only be bought in the best stores and were more expensive because they were superior. Radio appealed to a mass market that was wrong for Arden cosmetics. And sponsoring a radio show was an expensive proposition.

Other Arden executives tried to tell her the same thing, but she thought she knew better and signed a contract. She had objections to the show from the beginning. The gossip columnist would say unflattering things about Arden clients, and Elizabeth couldn't stop it because the network produced the show and she only footed the bill. It was a frustrating exercise for her and after her contract ran out, she withdrew as a sponsor. It had cost the company $200,000.

The independent Elizabeth began to do really silly things. Her good instincts for picking potential employees were not foolproof, although they had served her well in the past. Now she became foolhardy about them, too.

She asked one of her executives to investigate an individual she thought might be a useful addition to the company. When her employee reported some unsavory facts about the person in question, she fired the trusted employee and hired the outsider.

In the first two years following her separation from Tom Lewis, Elizabeth Arden went through five managers and lost $500,000 in her United States operations.

At last, she turned to her top advisers. Who, she asked, were the best managers in the business? They decided she was ready to listen, and they told her the truth. The best managers now all worked for Helena Rubinstein, and it would cost Elizabeth Arden plenty to entice them away. Not only would they want more money, but they would also require long-term contracts. Her reputation for not being able to hold onto employees was hurting her.

Elizabeth was in trouble and she knew it. But she also knew she couldn't afford not to hire the best people now, no matter how expensive they were.

And so the raiding wars began between the two cosmetic queens. Over the next several years, Elizabeth Arden—at great cost—took on eleven of Madame Rubinstein's top executives and started to turn around her American business.

She lost some employees herself in the raiding wars. Perhaps the most painful to her personally was Tom Lewis. Five years to the date of her dismissing him, he reentered the cosmetics business as an executive for Helena Rubinstein.

Perhaps he was by then an exhausted man. Perhaps the times were simply changing too fast for a man entering his sixties to follow. Whatever the reason, Tom Lewis never produced for Helena Rubinstein the remarkable results he had for Elizabeth Arden.

A Queen and the Sport of Kings

Wh* hen Elizabeth Arden was
the subject of a *Time* magazine cover story in 1946,
her cosmetics empire was not the issue. Horse racing
was. Under her portrait by artist Boris Chaliapin, the
caption read: "A queen rules the sport of kings."

From the days of her childhood when six-year-
old Florence Graham had been assigned the job of
helping her father with his shabby thoroughbreds,
Elizabeth Arden had adored horses. As a busy cosmetics executive building up a business, she had
neither the time nor the opportunity to pursue this
early love.

But in the flush of her success in the early 1930s,
she and Tom had been invited to Saratoga, New
York, one summer for the racing season. One of the
oldest and loveliest race tracks in America, Saratoga

attracted the cream of the New York racing world, which also was the cream of old New York society. Belmonts, Whitneys, Vanderbilts, and Paysons raced their horses at Saratoga.

The first summer there, Elizabeth caught the eye of Samuel D. Riddle, owner of the legendary Man-o'-War, one of the greatest American race-horses. In his three years on the track, the animal came in second only once. He won all his other races.

Riddle saw something tough and winning in Elizabeth that he liked. He told her he would be her mentor in racing, if the hobby appealed to her. Elizabeth was flattered, but reluctant at first. Having a hobby sounded like playing to her, and she didn't know how to play just for the fun of it. However, the more she saw of the racing scene, the more she liked it.

She bought her first thoroughbred in 1931 and won a $1,440 purse with it at Aqueduct, a race track on Long Island. The meager prize money barely covered the animal's keep, but Elizabeth had been bitten by the horse racing bug.

Little by little her new hobby became a bigger and bigger part of her life. She joined the Belmont and Saratoga racing associations and rented horse barns in both places.

As her marriage dissolved, her interest in the sport grew. It affected her business judgment, but not always adversely. When Gladys sent her samples of a new perfume she had discovered—the work of a chemist Gladys had uncovered in the south of France—Elizabeth agreed that it was wonderful and refreshing. To the consternation of her staff, she named the perfume "Blue Grass" for the famous horse-breeding region of Kentucky and Tennessee.

Her executives were afraid the horsey name would put women off. But Elizabeth again proved to have the better instincts. It became the best-selling perfume her company ever offered. And it helped support her new interest.

Her hobby needed heavy support in the early years. Her stables ran in the red for seven years before she was able to turn them into an asset. Luckily, Swanson came up with Elizabeth Arden's most successful product during that period—a soothing, healing lotion called Eight Hour Cream.

Elizabeth Arden was not a conventional horse owner, despite Sam Riddle's tutelage. Her horses became her babies, and she talked to them as one might address a very young child. She also insisted on treating them with Arden products. The Eight Hour Cream was actually a good liniment, and some trainers used it on the sly even after they left her employ.

She was as autocratic and difficult to work for in racing as she was in the beauty business, but she got trainers to take on her horses by offering fair wages and a guarantee of a year's pay.

For some old hands around the track, her approach was hard to swallow. She picked rosy pink, white, and blue as her racing colors, but she didn't confine them to her silks. She painted her barns in her colors, too. She also decorated them with hanging plants and had soothing music piped in for her "darlings," as she called her horses.

For all her silliness, she did institute some practices later that became standard procedure in racing stables. It was she who figured out that a good massage would be beneficial to a thoroughbred's legs before and after a race, for example.

She went through six trainers in six years. Then Louis Fuestal, who had trained Man-o'-War for Riddle, came to her. During his first year on the job, her barn at the Belmont track on Long Island burned down, killing three of her thoroughbreds. To rebuild her stock, he helped her buy a yearling named Great Union, a grandson of Man-o'-War. In 1939, as a three-year-old, Great Union won Elizabeth her first major stakes victory at Saratoga and finally put her stable in the black.

Elizabeth Arden with "Jewel's Reward," one of her top thoroughbreds, in 1958. She found racing stimulating and relaxing.

She had already put Elizabeth Arden back in the black after Tom's departure. She had added hair styling and manicures to the salon menu. She introduced a line of cosmetics for women with sensitive skin.

Elizabeth was indignant at the regulations imposed upon her industry by President Roosevelt's administration. But that was a matter of principle, not a specific problem for her company.

Cosmetics had been put under the Federal Drug Administration (FDA) for regulation. Products without FDA approval could not be offered for sale. Elizabeth resented the governmental interference, but her preparations had always been carefully monitored and tested in her own factories and were never called into question by the government. "My standards have always been higher than theirs," she told the press.

The Federal Trade Commission (FTC) took a dim view of some of the selling tactics used by cosmetics companies, which they felt were unfair trade practices. But, here again, the Elizabeth Arden company, which hired, trained, and paid its own saleswomen and demonstrators, was not affected.

New taxes on cosmetics did annoy Elizabeth, but she managed to pass the burden onto customers all the while she was complaining. She also protested the FTC insistence that she not make claims in advertising that she could not back up with scientific proof. She had to change some of her ad copy to comply, but she lost very little, if any, business.

As war clouds began to gather again over Europe in the late 1930s, Elizabeth took a shrewd, long-range view of her company. She had already opened salons in the major cities of South America, a backup source of income if war broke out in Europe and stopped business there. She kept a close watch on the South American outlets for her products. And she began stockpiling ingredients for her manufacturing plants. She knew that if the war spread, the government would get priority access to the raw materials she needed.

Her greatest concern was for her sister in Paris. Gladys insisted on staying with her husband in France. Elizabeth could not persuade her to do otherwise. Elizabeth did manage to help other Arden employees get out of occupied countries, and she supported a number of war refugees who made it to the United States.

When the United States entered the war, Elizabeth offered classes at night for women who had to enter the work force to take the place of the men who had gone to war. Held at the salon, they covered everything from diet and exercise to how to dress for the office.

In 1942 Elizabeth Arden, the hardheaded businesswoman, shocked all her friends and associates by marrying a penniless refugee Russian, Prince Michael Evlanoff. He was, evidently, a charming escort during their courtship, but Elizabeth was sixty-four-years old and she should have known better.

In the mid-1930s, Helena Rubinstein had married a titled Russian émigré, Prince Archil Gourielli-Tchkonka. She had set him up with his own line of men's cosmetics, the House of Gourielli. He was not a businessman, but he survived as a husband until his death in 1956.

Madame Rubinstein's new title—Princess Gourielli—may have been Elizabeth's inspiration. But Elizabeth soon learned that the title was too expensive, and she and her prince were separated within the year.

She returned to her cosmetics and thoroughbred businesses. At Elizabeth Arden, she decided that the war would destroy the Parisian leadership in fashion design and that it was time for her to get seriously into *haute couture*.

She tested the waters during the war by inviting her friend Charles James to do an exclusive line for the salons. He worked feverishly to create the designs and pick the fabrics for their first showing. The press gave excellent reviews, but Elizabeth Arden took all the credit for herself. James found that Elizabeth's highhandedness made it too difficult for them to work together. He also felt he had not made enough money from the deal to try it again.

Elizabeth was not discouraged. She was looking to the future and figured she could find younger, fresher talent elsewhere. She felt that she could offer a springboard for these untried designers into the world of fashion. They would be happy for the chance to show off what they could do.

She was right, and Elizabeth Arden did launch the careers of Antonio Castillo, Ferdinando Sarmi, and Oscar de la Renta.

The world of horse racing also was changing. Betting machines were being installed on the tracks. This allowed the race tracks to take a percentage of the gambling proceeds and raise the size of their purses to attract the best horses. For the first time, the sport of kings was beginning to pay off handsomely for smart owners.

When betting was handled strictly by bookmakers, almost all the race tracks ran at a loss, and racing associations had to help them out. Horse racing was then a game for the very rich. As Elizabeth became more and more involved, she recognized that she was pioneering another new industry.

She named her stables Maine Chance and continued to run them like beauty salons. The stableboys referred to her behind her back as "Mrs. Mudpack." Louis Fuestal retired, and she ran through another series of trainers. Some objected to using her products on the horses; others rebelled at the decor of the stables.

Then she hired "Silent" Tom Smith, an independent man who had spent the early part of his life knocking around in a series of jobs from cowhand to blacksmith. He had turned to horse training late. But he had picked out an unimpressive yearling and turned him into the unbeatable Seabiscuit. He was nearly seventy when he came to work for Elizabeth, but his reputation was still intact.

Smith just didn't talk much. He would hear Elizabeth out without comment. He put up with her strange ideas and funny ways, as long as he thought they didn't hurt the horses. "I try not to hurt her feelings, and yet do it my way," he said.

She grew to trust him. She bought the horses he recommended, and she raced them in the stakes races he thought they could win. The stable's earnings began to rise dramatically. In 1945, Maine Chance was the highest-winning stable in the United States.

In 1946 Elizabeth had three horses entered in the Kentucky Derby. This famous race for three-year-olds is held every May at Churchill Downs in Louisville. It is the first and most prestigious event in the Triple Crown of racing.

Two of Elizabeth's horses were the bettors' favorites to win. A week before the race, the Derby entries were already in Kentucky. The rest of her horses—twenty-eight expensive thoroughbreds—were in her stable at Arlington Park, a race track in Chicago.

Shortly after midnight, the nightwatchman at Arlington Park smelled smoke. He opened the door of an unoccupied box stall, and flames shot out. The terrified man sounded an alarm and raced to wake up the stablehands to help him rescue the horses.

It proved to be one of the costliest fires in racing history, and its cause was never determined. Twenty-two of Elizabeth's thoroughbreds and two lead ponies died. Only six horses were saved. She had them trucked to Kentucky immediately.

Insurance did not begin to cover Elizabeth's loss. Nor did her favorites in the Derby. Neither of them won. When reporters asked her what she planned to do, she said gamely, "I think I better buy some new horses."

A Queen and the Sport of Kings

She did, of course. But this wasn't necessary to win the Derby. One of the horses saved from the fire was a two-year-old named Jet Pilot. He had been brought to Kentucky the day after the disaster. Tom Smith suggested that they put him in a race for two-year-olds at Churchill Downs on Derby Day.

It was the first race of the day and Jet Pilot's racing debut. He won by nine lengths. The next year he brought Elizabeth great pleasure by winning the 1947 Kentucky Derby.

Standing in the winner's circle on that happy day, she must have thought of her father and his dream of such a moment.

Arden congratulates jockey Bobby Permane, after his win in the Santa Anita Derby in 1946, riding her horse "Knockdown."

Elizabeth Arden liked to win in the beauty business and the horse business. The competition kept her going in both arenas, and she never flagged.

Nor did she ever mellow. When her dominance of the cosmetics industry was challenged by the aggressive marketing tactics of a Boston entrepreneur named Charles Revson, she simply referred to him as "that man."

Revson's company, Revlon, gave all the established cosmetics companies competition with his heavy advertising campaigns and his provocative product names. He made a fortune pushing hundreds of shades of nail polish and matching lipsticks into a mass market.

Selling cosmetics door to door gave the Avon company an advantage that took profits away from the Arden company.

Most threatening of all was Estée Lauder, a young woman from Queens, New York, who started selling a new face cream by giving demonstrations to women in hair salons, then department stores. A

Elizabeth Arden greets Senator Everett Dirkson of Illinois at a reception she gave during the Republican Convention of 1956.

supersaleswoman, she produced good products and packaged them with distinction. And she seemed to have a gift for training her salespeople in her techniques.

Elizabeth Arden should have admired the determination and drive that kept this new entrant in the field going. Estée Lauder was carefully building a successful beauty empire based on the same ideas of quality and imaginative good taste that had made Elizabeth Arden so profitable.

She couldn't. Elizabeth, visiting in Paris, discovered one afternoon that Estée Lauder was downstairs in the Arden salon having her hair done. It was the only salon open on Mondays, and Mrs. Lauder wanted to look her best for a dinner with the Duke and Duchess of Windsor. Elizabeth flew into a rage, accused her competitor of spying, and threw her out.

Elizabeth Arden could not retire from either of her businesses. She continued to run her cosmetics company and her horses like an energetic dictator until the day she died in 1966. She was 88 years old and had outlived Helena Rubinstein by a year.

Elizabeth Arden had always thrived on her active and independent involvement in the running of her business. She had never considered stepping down, slowing down—or dying. Although her will made provisions for generous bequests to her sister Gladys, a niece, a nephew, and her employees (including a chauffeur who had named his daughter Ardena), it did not deal with a transition of leadership within the cosmetics company or the racing stables.

After four years of litigation, her properties— houses all over the world, art works, and horses— were sold and the cosmetics empire was bought by a giant pharmaceutical company, Eli Lilly.

Lilly continues to develop and market beauty products under the Elizabeth Arden name. The packaging is still pink, and the doors to the remaining salons are still red.

Bibliography

Allen, Margaret. *Selling Dreams: Inside the Beauty Business.* New York: Simon and Schuster, 1981.

Ash, Mary Kay. *Mary Kay.* New York: Harper and Row, 1981.

Banner, Lois W. *American Beauty.* New York, Alfred A. Knopf, 1983.

Corson, Richard. *Fashions in Makeup from Ancient to Modern Times.* Chester Springs, Pa.; Dufour, 1972.

Lauder, Estee. *Estee: A Success Story.* New York: Random House, 1985.

Lewis, Alfred A. and Constance Woodworth. *Miss Elizabeth Arden: An Unretouched Portrait.* New York: Coward, McCann Geoghegan, Inc., 1972.

Schwartz, Hillel. *Never Satisfied: A Cultural History of Diets, Fantasies and Fat.* New York: Macmillan, 1986.

Time-Life Books (ed.). *This Fabulous Century.* Alexandria, Va.: Time-Life Books, 1974.

White, Frederick Allen. *Only Yesterday.* New York: Harper and Brothers, 1931.

Wykes-Jones, Max. *Cosmetics and Adornment.* New York: Philosophical Library, 1961.

Index

stock market crash, 89–90
Swanson, A. Fabian, 69, 70–71, 73, 79, 99

T

Tadd, Mrs. (great-aunt), 12, 15
Tadd, Samuel (great grandfather), 9
Tennyson, Alfred, Lord, 42
Time (magazine), 97
Titus, Edward J., 79
Toronto, Ontario, 9–10, 11, 13, 17, 18, 19, 21, 22, 24, 32
tuberculosis, 11

V

"Venetian" products, 47, 61, 62, 68, 70, 73, 74
Venice, Italy, 47–48
Venus de Milo, 38
Victoria (queen of England), 8
Vienna, Austria, 63, 64
Vienna Youth Mask, 92
Vogue (magazine), 39, 53, 60, 74, 79

W

Waldorf Astoria Hotel, 49
Walker, A'lelia, 76
Walker, Mrs. C.J., 74, 75, 75, 76
Wanamaker's (department store), 26
Washington, D.C., 62, 63, 71
Whistler, James McNeill, 36
Wilde, Oscar, 88
Windsor, Duchess of, 107
Windsor, Duke of, 107
women's occupations, 16, 17, 18, 76, 102
women's suffrage, 43, *59*, 59–60
Woodbridge, Ontario, 6, 7, 10, 17, 19, 20, 23, 27, 30
World Famed Princess Tonic Hair Restorer, 20
World War I, 63, 66, 67, 72, 73, 77, 79, 81, 85
World War II, 101, 102

Y

Yardley (cosmetics co.), 83

Acknowledgments and Credits

Frontispiece and pages 29, 82, UPI/Bettmann Newsphotos.

Pages 13, 16, 27, 32–33, 58, 59, 72, Culver Pictures, Inc.

Pages 41, 44, 50–51, 54, 75, 85, 90–91, The Bettmann Archive.

Pages 79, 84, 100, 105, 106, AP/Wide World Photos.